2-23-73

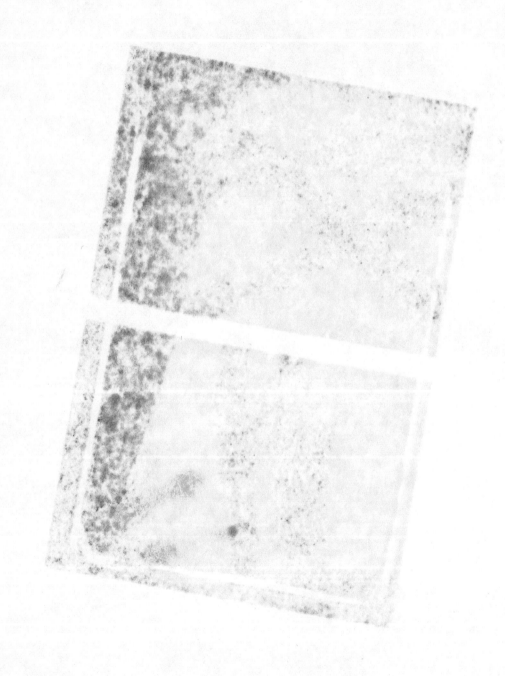

the new wedding

Photography by Ingbet

Alfred A. Knopf   New York   1973

thenewwedding

Creating your own marriage ceremony

Khoren Arisian

THIS IS A BORZOI BOOK PUBLISHED BY ALFRED A. KNOPF, INC.

Library of Congress Cataloging in Publication Data

Arisian, Khoren.   The new wedding.   Bibliography: p.   1. Marriage service.   I. Title.
BV199.M3A74 1973   265'.5   72–11029   ISBN 0–394–48334–0

Manufactured in the United States of America

to Peg, Christopher, and Derek

contents

acknowledgments

In putting this volume together I am especially indebted to Peg Arisian, my wife, whose sharply critical eye for essentials helped me to recast my original efforts with more precision; to Margaret J. Stephens, a good friend and crackerjack librarian whose brilliant bibliographical sleuthing proved invaluable and saved me countless hours; to Ruth Merr, my secretary, who typed an often complicated manuscript with patience and understanding; and to Toinette Rees, my editor, whom it was a pleasure to come to know and whose sensitive judgments were instrumental in bringing the various parts of the book into final balance.

I would be remiss not to mention, above all, Angus Cameron of Knopf. We first became acquainted almost a decade ago when I had the privilege of officiating at his son's wedding, and from that beginning a precious friendship has emerged. A man who always plays to people's strengths, Angus Cameron was unflagging in his special interest and encouragement of my inclinations to write. That interest has borne its first fruit.

Of course, this whole endeavor would have been inconceivable apart from the many wonderful young people who came to me at a crucial juncture of their lives—that time when a prospective unconditional commitment to another human being required a fresh religious and moral perception in the form of a humanistic wedding ceremony. In my interviews with a number of them I realized that something significant was happening. That significance—its sources and its implications—is what this book is all about. I am grateful to all these young people for their open and cooperative spirit, and extend special thanks to those whose ceremonial efforts appear in these pages in whole or in part.

KHOREN ARISIAN

New York City   February 1973

gettingmarriedtoday

It used to be that people got married as a matter of course. Little attention was paid to the ceremony itself, and even less to the nature of matrimony. Wedding customs were simply accepted and followed, while the ceremonies, for Protestants at least, were used verbatim or adapted from the Anglican Book of Common Prayer of 1662.

For a person not to get married was the unusual and daring course. If it was a woman, people thought of her as either an object of suspicion or a sad old maid; if it was a man, they assumed that he was headed for a career of moral and social irresponsibility. In short, moral commitment in marriage was considered subordinate to institutional needs, expression, and sanctification.

The Changing Attitude toward Marriage

Today, however, moral commitment is increasingly regarded as antecedent to and superior to institutional attempts to encompass it. We are in the midst of a pervasive and passionate criticism, in some cases a revulsion, against marriage as a kind of death trap for individual self-development. One recalls Colette's haunting, perceptive comments on how the institution of marriage has over the ages relentlessly inflicted its "small deaths" on both men and women. The new feminism of the 1970's has played a large part in bringing public attention to this aspect of wedlock.

No longer, then, do people feel quite the compulsion to get married sooner or later under conventional auspices. Men and women both can choose consciously not to get married and can look forward to a fulfilling life-style without it. People recognize more and more that the "happily ever after" myth has been one of humankind's grossest moral deceptions. Marriage requires daily attention, and children are a lot of hard work. As people become aware of these facts before marriage, it is more likely that they will enter upon it with fewer limiting preconceptions and an expanded capacity to make the most of its unique possibilities. Monogamous marriage, in other words, no longer has to be the great disillusionment, either a prison or a stopping point in a person's growth.

The Development of the Individual through Marriage

Any conjugal relationship dies from within when affection dries up. For it is the nature of truly mutual love to generate the equality of those loving each other—and this miracle can happen more or less in any period of history. Today it is more likely to happen than ever before: love, we are learning, somehow liberates the potential for morality, even as no moral can be derived from love except the injunction to love better.

"Who knows of the possibilities of love," asks Betty Friedan in *The Feminine Mystique*, "when men and women share not only children, home, and garden, not only the fulfillment of their biological roles, but the responsibilities and passions of the work that creates the human future and the full human knowledge of who they are?" This is perhaps the underlying message communicated by the New Wedding. No personal moral growth is possible without an equal relationship. When Nora in Ibsen's *A Doll's House* (probably the first modern classic treatment of women's rights) tells Thorvald that no marriage can be built on ultimate inequality between the sexes, she is enunciating what, for the New Wedding, is a moral necessity. Nora feels she must be a whole person, a woman, in marriage, or else it is no deal—and in the tight Victorian world of the 1890's she had no choice but to walk out on an impossible marriage.

The marriage relationship is among the most intense of experiences, but its intensity will burn away rather than multiply the convergent energies of the partners if equality is not its mainspring. For too long women have allowed marriage as a dependency-fostering institution to depress their opportunities; for too long men have accepted this unnatural burden. No one can live another's life; no one can live for another person exclusively and not become spiritually dehydrated.

We can come to enjoy another person more as we make room for our own development. Fulfillment does not spring from self-abnegation but from caring for another's needs in the light of our own.

Equality between Husband and Wife

Community, which is what marriage is all about, is conceived of as a communion of individual wills. Distance between people is a given fact; love must respect that distance. The partners to an approaching marriage are urged to be guardians of each other's solitude, for without solitude no deeply satisfying social existence is possible.

Of course, the conventional belief persists that marriage will and should dissolve the distance between two people. This is the morally corrosive myth that the partners will some-

how become "one flesh," an enriched unity. What it means historically is that the wife has been expected to subordinate her will and individuality to her husband's; it is her, rather than his, distinctiveness that has normally been sacrificed.

Annexation of one partner by another can only diminish both and is by definition unethical; unlike Mies van der Rohe's architectural law of parsimony, this is one case where less is not more. The New Wedding is virtually a moral proclamation, even a protest, against any sort of annexation in marriage; it is a ceremonial microcosm of one's growing vision of oneself and of the world beyond. There is room here only for growth that is mutually enhancing; the growth of one person at the expense of another is contradictory and self-canceling. Genuine love may be described as the passionate, abiding desire on the part of two people to generate together the conditions under which each can be, and can express, his/her real self.

Social Responsibility A second major point is that marriage does not absolve the person from larger social responsibilities. Indeed, a few young people who are social idealists sometimes will conceive of a lyrical socialist ceremony, stating that what they do together in the world for humanity is more important than what they do together privately or alone. But social existence has a personal side, and personal existence has a social side; this balance must be kept in view. Social responsibility should not be used as an excuse to evade love's legitimate demands, yet love is not love which is centered on itself alone. Whatever success in marriage may connote, it has less to do with finding the right person than with being the right person.

Marriage on the Increase Since it is currently so easy to engage in liaisons without formal bonds, it requires more than a slight mutual commitment for a couple to want to get married. Marriage is no longer so necessary as it used to be for gaining economic security, social respectability, or regular sexual satisfaction. Marriages none-theless continue to increase: well over two million take place every year. The point is that marriage is hardly disappearing so much as attitudes toward it are changing rapidly and rad-ically. We should not be surprised that the wedding ceremony, which (whatever its character) celebrates the advent of mar-riage, is also undergoing rapid change. In many ways, today is a remarkably exciting and challenging time to get married.

The Need for the New Wedding

By any measure the New Wedding is a singular phenomenon: as a cultural development it has no immediately discernible antecedents. New Weddings are multiplying for the obvious reason that the old weddings no longer adequately meet human needs. Not that the old ceremonies do not retain some-thing of the human feelings behind a decision to marry; they do. But traditional ceremonies carry too little of what is felt these days about the coming together of two human beings in marriage. By contrast the New Wedding expresses a very personal and timely urgency; in its ambience and content it exemplifies continuity through change. What we need to do is to see what the connection is between the rise of the New Weddings and the recent evolution of marriage in the Western world.

In the West, marriage has been classically regarded as a sacrament in which the contracting parties are ministers to each other. Solemnization in front of a priest or rabbi is a much later emergence. And even with the presence of an of-ficiant, the couple still marry themselves to each other: this is what makes the new partnership morally real and spiritually valid. This does not render it legal, however, for the state's authorization comes only with the conduct of the wedding by a minister—or the required legality can be conferred in briefer form by a judge or justice of the peace, leaving the couple free to marry themselves in any ceremonial manner they choose.

The difference is that in the past, couples did not normally avail themselves of this freedom. Nobody reminded them of the essence of the Western religious tradition, nor was there the open cultural climate which today stirs people to be more aware of their own powers and of the right to exercise them. When was this climate created?

In the 1960's a virtual quantum leap in consciousness occurred throughout much of the world. Vatican II was held. A death-of-God theology sensationally appeared and vanished, leaving a considerable residue of awareness concerning the importance of human initiative in religious thinking and belief. The "new morality" both accompanied and succeeded the death-of-God flurry. Its essence was the notion of love as conscience-in-action expressed as rational decision-making in specific contexts. Most "new morality" discussions centered upon mutual human needs and loosened uptight conceptions and practices relating to love, sex, and marriage. As Simone de Beauvoir had long since observed in *The Second Sex:* "In a genuinely moral erotic relation there is free assumption of desire and pleasure, or at least a moving struggle to regain liberty in the midst of sexuality; but this is possible only when the other is recognized *as an individual*, in love or in desire."

Inevitably, the wedding ceremony itself was profoundly affected. By the end of the decade the New Wedding came into full view. Indeed, on July 1, 1969, the Catholic Church made at least a symbolic concession to the uncommon spirit: the Vatican on that date promulgated a liberalized liturgy, including some altered marriage vows. A choice of thirty readings from the Bible could now be used instead of the usual epistle and gospel in the existing nuptial mass.

Apart from the ferment within the religious realm, two other potent factors in the development of the New Wedding were the growth of a many-layered counterculture, mostly youthful (the overwhelming majority of New Weddings are conducted by young clergy for young couples); and the explosive emergence of the new feminism, which is rapidly taking up the unfinished work of the early feminist movement.

The Influence
of Women's Liberation

The increasingly equalitarian views about sex relations and alternative life-styles on the part of many counter-conventional young men and women have gradually seeped into contemporary consciousness. Enlarging and giving that consciousness a moral imperative has been the surge of Women's Liberation.

The first women's rights convention in the United States was held at Seneca Falls, New York, in 1848. A landmark gathering, the convention adopted a number of resolutions calling for the general liberation of women. Finding the prevailing situation ethically and legally intolerable, the feminist movement slowly, at great cost, gained ground over a century and at last attained national suffrage in 1920. But even though these gains opened up opportunities for a meaningful life outside marriage and greater dignity within it, they did not eliminate cultural biases on behalf of men's freer behavior and women's restriction to bedroom and kitchen. A woman in nineteenth- and early twentieth-century England or America simply had no legal status apart from her husband. She could not vote or own property. If she was not married she did not even have derivative legal protection. English common law recognized only the man, in whose person the wife was considered legally subsumed. In a court of law to this day, a wife and husband are not normally allowed to testify against each other if one is accused of a felony, so much are they presumed to be "one flesh"; the principle of protection against self-incrimination can be invoked here.

Through the 1950's and into the early 1960's the single woman in America was still motivated to get married as soon as possible—almost, it would seem, in order to continue belonging to someone. Even in many otherwise up-to-date ceremonies, the notion of women as chattels survives in the minister's question to the father: "Who gives this woman to be married to this man?" Semantic upgrading of the question to "Who presents the bride?" does not fully conceal matters. Why, after all, should the bride be singled out for presentation?

Meanwhile, the society pages of most newspapers phrase their reports so that the woman is "married to" the man. Further evidence of the pervasive sexist approach occurs in the single-ring ceremony, in which the man places the ring on the bride's finger. This harks back to the ancient capture of the bride, who was secured by a large metal ring placed usually around her ankle to prevent her from escaping: she was her husband's possession.

The Women's Liberation Movement is addressing itself vigorously to both the subtle and the visible penalties and put-downs, the psychological and mythological roots of remaining sexual inequality. The patriarchal assumptions of Western society clearly go very deep. Yet these assumptions are being frontally assaulted as people increasingly demand more fulfilling forms of social and political order than they have known, and as they insist on participating more directly in decisions that affect them. One of these is the choice today to have a New Wedding.

Until quite recently marriage was regarded as something of a triumph for the woman and a loss for the man. What purpose, among others, has the dowry signified if not that of discreet compensation of the bridegroom for the bride—for taking her over from her family and henceforth supporting her? Marriage was the woman's trophy, the ultimate test of her seductive capacities, her admission card to security and behind-the-scenes influence. But for the man it was a snare and a burden, as much popular folk humor indicates. Man was caught, not liberated, in marriage: the restless wanderer caged, civilized, and cared for by "the woman of the house."

Ironically, however, while the man *felt* trapped, the woman actually *was* trapped. She was locked firmly into place, pledged by the traditional wedding vow "to love, honor and obey." This mutually unfair arrangement led to the unnecessary anguish of dead-end marriages as depicted, for instance, in Leo Tolstoy's *Anna Karenina* and *The Kreutzer Sonata*, and in D. H. Lawrence's *Lady Chatterley's Lover*.

Such intolerable tension eventually had to be resolved by the emergence in our time of more flexible and open patterns of marriage. And as these new patterns appear, people begin to demand that they be given social recognition and legal respectability.

The Legal Status of Husband and Wife

Traditional legal obligations are simply not alterable through informal agreements, however specific. Certain understandings, even if written, between a husband and wife have only so much moral force as each partner grants them. They are not binding in a court of law—at least, not yet. Recent congressional passage of the Equal Rights Amendment portends eventual alterations in attitudes. Today some people, including some lawyers, feel that a couple should have the legally recognized right to make any monogamic marriage contract they wish to negotiate.

Woman's own insistence on independence both within and without marriage has forced a change in traditional assumptions. Of all the institutions we have surrounded ourselves with, marriage is among the most rigid and the last to change. And not until marriage began to be fundamentally reassessed could the wedding ceremony itself be fashioned anew.

At the same time that this fundamental reassessment of marriage has been negative and analytical, occasionally tending toward brilliant overkill, it has helped to reveal the singular possibilities for renewal and growth that the experience of marriage can offer. At the end of her monumental book, *The Second Sex*, Simone de Beauvoir prophesied, "The free woman is just being born." She is also, preeminently in America today, beginning to flower in her greater freedom. In the long run this development will help liberate men from their own shackles. The New Wedding bases itself on the possibility of reciprocal moral and personal growth. Why cannot mar-

11

riage and the New Wedding that celebrates it be an equal triumph for man and woman?

Insofar as it announces the coming of mutual liberation, the New Wedding serves to express the moral revolution of our time. Candor is the New Wedding's psychological keynote; consciousness, self-awareness, is its spiritual keynote; equality is its moral keynote.

This book is a partial record of the ceremonial ways in which changing attitudes toward love and matrimony are manifested. As a permanent institution marriage is dignified and strengthened by ceremonial observance. Only in stagnant times does such observance become archaic, absurd, and worthy of satire. But in times of change, ceremonial observance becomes even more pertinent and vital as it expresses the dynamics of the day.

In the chapters that follow, the wedding is conceived of as a humanistic celebration for our time. Enrichment of the individual identity of each partner is deemed superior to concern for the usual social roles and expectations.

This book is written not only as a resource for those contemplating a "new" marriage ceremony, but also for the general reader who may be interested in learning how a new moral consciousness can emerge from the turbulence of the day— and how this consciousness can be shaped into rational expression at a significant point in people's lives.

thenatureof
thenewwedding

It has been said that weddings are getting out of hand these days, which means they are becoming newsworthy. No longer is the dullest writing in the newspaper necessarily found in the society section; there we hear of weddings in Central Park, of brides going barefoot in the grass, of grooms wearing garlands. It is not really that weddings are getting out of hand so much as that they are becoming radically different in their moral approach, as well as more colorful in form and in content.

What Is a New Wedding? Many people who contemplate marriage today do not want their ceremony to be saturated with abstract, Platonic statements that have no relationship to human reality and ability; they do not want merely to go through the expected motions; they do not want to be weighted down in the ceremony itself with heavy psychic and social responsibilities. In short, they choose candor rather than the well-meant hypocrisy of the old weddings. The more serious among them will avoid ceremonies containing pointless language that is sometimes used by various "hip" clergymen—for example, "Do you promise to stick together so long as you both shall dig it?" Marriage is a serious business, however one approaches it. Treating it flippantly and treating it sanctimoniously are two sides of the same spurious coin.

By the New Wedding I mean that kind of ceremony where the attempt is made, through words and gestures, to present an honest personal view of human relationships in today's world. Often this view is an assertion of the so-called liberated consciousness that refuses to be bound by social conventions devoid of persuasive rationality. More often it is an expression of the growing nonsectarian humanist sensibility which acknowledges life as continuous process and permutation. Ritual as simple repetition invariably makes words and ideas meaningless. People must participate in the ceremonies that underscore their mutual obligations: in this way they are more likely to abide by them.

A conscious sense of the personal as the most real is intensified in periods of history when social institutions are felt to be working against human beings more than on their behalf. So the New Wedding is characteristically imbued with an individualistic spirit. Marriage, to be genuine, must be a private, personal choice, and the two persons involved have to accept and work through whatever consequences the choice may bring.

Confirming an Existing Relationship

Couples genuinely in love are already emotionally married to each other before they are finally wed. The New Wedding ceremony may take note of this fact in a variety of ways. It must somehow embody an awareness that no ceremony creates human relationships but only recognizes what has developed. Living together before marriage, which is so common these days as to go unnoticed, may or may not help to advance the process of mutual understanding. In any event, such a practice cannot be dismissed with righteous moralism— it is far too complex. The new sensibility recognizes that it is not impossible for sex relations as a reasonable and caring activity, in which the whole personality is spontaneously involved, to occur outside marriage.

During the 1920's, as he viewed the shipwrecked marriages that came into his court, Judge Benjamin Lindsey of Denver, Colorado, felt there had to be a better way—something involving more open monogamous patterns. So he proposed "companionate marriage," which a couple would have the power to dissolve relatively easily. This became a subject for national controversy, and Lindsey eventually lost his judgeship owing to political pressures. Bertrand Russell found Lindsey's conception eminently reasonable. And because he too advocated trial marriage, Russell was prevented from teaching at the College of the City of New York in 1940. Young people, Lindsey had argued, should have the free choice to marry and, by practicing birth control, avoid having children for an unspecified period. If no children were forthcoming, divorce should be obtainable by mutual consent and alimony should not be allowed. Of course, what Judge Lindsey advocated as a lawful possibility has today become a common informal practice without legal guidelines.

Indeed, a few couples go so far as to state in the ceremony itself that as a result of living together for a while, they have decided that they wish to legalize their union for an indefinite period. Be that as it may, a wedding ceremony is an important outward acknowledgment of a more important inward communion of mind and spirit. It connotes the end of a beginning and marks a new beginning. Neither the state nor religious

institutions can make any legitimate moral claim to creating, sanctifying, or annulling a marriage. The legal and the moral are never wholly identical: laws may perpetuate injustices, while moral practices may not enjoy social sanction or legal protection.

The overt act of union, the wedding ceremony, which celebrates the beginning of a new relationship between human beings, thus represents an opportunity for a couple to declare openly and coherently their personal feelings upon arriving at what is perhaps life's most critical juncture. For these two people who have chosen each other out of the whole human race are now ready to promise to transcend their egos sufficiently to enter into one another's experience and care for each other in exceptional ways.

The Attitudes behind the Ceremony

"Doing your thing," within the wedding context, means shaping the words and ambience of the ceremony itself with the professional aid of a clergyman. A minister who performs a purely priestly role (that is, humbly does what he is asked to do, whether it is requested by a religious institution or by an individual, without somehow putting himself into it) is violating his own integrity.

People who seek a humanistic marriage ceremony have usually decided that they want neither the barrenness of a justice-of-the-peace ritual nor the predictable sanctification of one of the usual religious faiths. They want instead a ceremony that respects their personal feelings, that takes note of their distinctiveness and capacity for judgment. They are ready to admit that they will make their own lives and that their marriage will be shaped not in some heaven or utopia, but from the resources of their own fallible humanity in space and time.

Many young people these days are unwilling to exchange vows to stay married "till death do us part." They witness the high rate of divorce and the emotional wrenching it entails, and they wish to be more humble in both their initial and their long-range expectations. They prefer, that is, to take one year at a time. They are not ready to assume vast abstract obligations prior to experience; they believe that obligations should increase naturally as people experience one another.

In many of the New Weddings, the affirmation of the personal in terms of simplicity and directness is bound up with an enthusiastic attitude toward nature, as well as a more or less critical view of contemporary social institutions. A number of New Weddings have a natural setting—under the trees, on a beach, on a hillside, beside a lake. This return to the outdoors mirrors a renewed sense of the moral connection that ought to exist between the human and the natural. Many young people feel that formal society frequently fails to provide genuine community—that they must seek social community largely outside traditional institutions, and must find further renewal and compensation in the community between the individual and nature.

With varying degrees of integrity and confusion, New Weddings reflect the view that much of the creative possibility of life today, much of "the action," is found outside, around, and despite institutions. These weddings represent an antiauthoritarian espousal of the right to find one's meaning where one can.

Composing the Ceremony The ceremony for a New Wedding should mirror as closely as possible the feelings and beliefs of the couple, but its form and content must be easily understood by the guests. Composing an original ceremony is an act of creation. The need, desire, and attempt to do so help to focus and renew the couple's essential feelings about each other and their own selves. The primary purpose of this book, however, is not to delineate the step-by-step process of writing a New Wedding but to present the reader with a variety of ceremonies that have already attempted to come to terms with the challenge.

The New Wedding by definition begins with the individual, not with society's demands; it begins with feelings explored and talked through prior to final public utterance. For if a couple start with familiar and given words, with liturgical convention, they will probably muddy the meaning of what they uniquely believe it takes to share their lives with one another. They are therefore encouraged to construct their New Wedding by taking conscious note of their feelings about themselves, including their reservations, and what effect those feelings may have on the future of the relationship. Love between people is knowable to the extent that it is direct and honest. If it is to be real, a wedding must grow out of the reality of the relationship it announces. The marriage ceremony is virtually the first and last public, rational acknowledgment of that intended relationship.

Whenever people bypass current conventions in favor of a direct, simple way of doing things, they often unknowingly revive the most humane aspects of a tradition and bring them into a contemporary milieu. The search for pertinence having begun with a person's own felt humanity—which can be a surprisingly accurate plumb line to ancient origins that are humanely simple—external innovations within given norms can and should easily follow.

For example, if a couple contemplating marriage want the ceremony to be held outdoors because upon reflection it makes natural and human sense, they reiterate a sentiment and practice going back thousands of years. In the farthest recesses of Hebrew culture (before the Babylonian exile of the sixth century B.C.) weddings normally took place under the heavens. As Judaism subsequently moved from temple to synagogue, so did the Jewish wedding move indoors and under the *huppah* within the synagogue. Originally the *huppah* was the chamber where the bride received the groom for consummation of their marriage following the end of the betrothal period. This bridal chamber eventually served as a model for the cloth canopy stretched across four poles beneath which the Jewish wedding has traditionally been solemnized.

How are innovations made within given norms? A couple's creation of their own wedding materials entirely afresh, or by splicing unfamiliar ingredients with old materials, is in keeping with that aspect of the Western marriage tradition which recognizes bride and groom as ministers to each other in the ceremony. The creative and radical extension of this free aspect of the tradition entails the personal participation of bride and groom in the ceremony's actual composition.

When a couple about to be married decide they want a New Wedding, they sometimes carry it out by themselves, with a judge or justice of the peace close by to legalize it. More commonly, however, they enlist the aid of a sympathetic clergyman who is himself a bit of a heretic. He may be from any religious background—no denomination has a monopoly on New Weddings. All three—officiant, bride, and groom—may work on the ceremony; even friends and members of the family may be invited to contribute. In the end, however, orchestration of its several parts will be the couple's own. Traditional phrases or sentiments from any of the conventional ceremonies may be mixed in with readings, say, from the writings of John Kennedy, Walt Whitman, Nikos Kazantzakis, or Kahlil Gibran (most of all), or from the *Upanishads* or the *I Ching* (the Chinese *Book of Changes*, a collection of propositions used in divination). In the last few years there has been an increasing interest in Eastern culture and religion, and more and more people are turning to Buddhist and Hindu scriptures in their search for a clear and simple approach to truth.

The New Weddings, while having much in common, thus can differ greatly in form and content. A few may assume a distinctly Eastern mystical stance. Most will be Western in tone; some will invoke a naturalistic mysticism; some will stress public obligation to the common good; some will underscore the many aspects of mutual care and devotion. What-

21

ever the emphasis, the overriding concern in almost all wedding ceremonies, old or new, is the nature of the relationship between a man and a woman in marriage.

Romance and Reality   The New Wedding is biased in favor of poetry, language, and ideas that have a strong orientation toward reality here and now. "People are only transformed when they participate in the transformation of reality," wrote Marxist critic George Lukacs. The New Wedding prepares the groundwork for transformation, for mutual growth, by its stress on reality. When the romantic emerges naturally from the real, it is suffused with an unmistakable integrity—as, for example, in these lines from Elizabeth Barrett Browning's Sonnet 14:

If thou must love me, let it be for nought
Except for love's sake only. Do not say,
"I love her for her smile—her look—her way
Of speaking gently—for a trick or thought
That falls in well with mine. . . ."
For these things in themselves, Beloved, may
Be changed, or change for thee—and love, so wrought,
May be unwrought so. . . .

The marriage of Robert Browning and Elizabeth Barrett is one of the most renowned romances in English literary history. It was through his admiration for her poetry that Browning met Elizabeth Barrett in 1845 when she was forty years old and languishing in an arbitrarily patriarchal home. Drawn swiftly and surely to each other, they had no choice in Victorian England but to elope—to Italy, where they enjoyed a married life that refreshed and deepened them both for the balance of their lives. Theirs proved to be a richly reciprocal relationship between two independent equals. Though this kind of conjugal experience is possible in any age, it was a very exotic exception in the last century. The New Wedding is fast ushering in the notion that a liberating experience in marriage can become the moral and emotional rule for those who choose it.

To sum up: the New Wedding is not discontinuous with the historical development of marriage in the Western world. On the contrary, it represents a fresh reshaping of some very old ingredients and attitudes that are biased in favor of the freedom and fulfillment of the individual. As such it radically returns to usable origins, not for imitation but for lively inspiration. Strengthened by its bonds with Western tradition, it moves forward to new frontiers in the present.

newweddingceremonies

the New Weddings described here all have been revised or re-created for the purposes of this volume. Portions of all have been used on one or more occasions. Most of the ceremonies are my own; in several instances they include material added by the bride and groom. Where a ceremony is substantially or completely someone else's, or where I have reworked it slightly, I have said so in the notes preceding it. Readers are welcome to incorporate the insights and phraseology into their own marriage statements. Even though a few of the weddings have some elements in common, their variations in language and emphasis render each ceremony unique.

But what makes each ceremony legal?

Any wedding is legal if, in addition to the required witnesses, a justice of the peace, a judge, or an authorized clergyman signs the wedding license. Issuance of a license gives public notice of the intent of matrimony. By the same token it invokes the protections and requirements of the laws pertaining to marriage and the family.

Despite the much-touted separation of church and state, the religious and civil provinces are in practice thoroughly

intertwined: whenever a duly ordained or otherwise certified clergyman conducts a marriage ceremony in the United States, he serves as an agent of the government.

This probably derives from the time of the Puritans who emigrated to the New World and settled in New England, for they maintained a civil rather than a sacramental view of marriage. But by the end of the seventeenth century, legal authorization for the performance of religious wedding ceremonies by ministers became the practice. In the Massachusetts Bay Colony, church and state were the same. Disestablishment did not come about until the early nineteenth century, and the consequent legal separation of church and state still did not alter the custom of marriages being legally performed by ministers of religion.

In many European countries, by contrast, a civil ceremony is distinct from and supersedes the religious ceremony. A civil ceremony alone is legally recognized, and the clergy are actually prohibited from performing a religious ceremony prior to the civil one.

What technically must be said by an officiant in any of the United States is minimal, differs from state to state, and can be expressed in a number of different ways. Legal requirements

need never be an obstacle to the spirit or scope of any wedding, old or new, since marriage is the consequence of the ceremony in its entirety rather than of any particular moment in it, including any pronouncement.

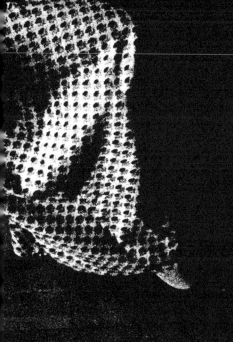

love through music

Since the New Wedding focuses on human feelings in their immediacy, the most appropriate music, if music is used at all, is that which embodies a direct expression of feelings. Certain kinds of rock are surprisingly relevant in the context of some New Weddings. In contrast, "Here Comes the Bride" and the traditional wedding march from Wagner's Lohengrin are altogether too public in impact. A wedding should be more an intimate than a state occasion. Theatrical music that insistently draws attention to itself rather than serving as a vehicle for feeling—including, for instance, much of Franz Liszt's music—should be avoided. Chopin's piano music, however, is superbly evocative of the kind of honest personal feeling which a wedding grows out of and should communicate. The question whether music at a wedding should be quiet or loud is unimportant. For specific suggestions, see Songs and Music, pages 147–151.

Concerto No. 1 for Piano and Orchestra—Frederic Chopin (Recorded selections may be played from the second movement, or the piano alone may be "live.")

OFFICIANT   Dear Friends, one of the poets of the piano was Frederic Chopin. In his music we find a virtual unveiling and spiritual delineation of the inner life. This sometimes borders on sentimentality but never crosses over into it. Chopin's piano music is one of mankind's supreme evocations of the spirit of tenderness and mutuality. As a company of witnesses who have converged at this point in space and time in order to rejoice with _____ and _____ in their coming together for the purpose of wedlock, we have been hearing together what Chopin has to say to us from his Concerto No. 1 for piano and orchestra.

It is tragically common for human beings to withhold from one another what is best, unique, excellent, in themselves. Since this is the spiritual part in all of us, it can only be lost or diminished from being withheld. To bring it out into the open, to expose it to sunlight and rain, to wrath and joy, is to increase its depth and extent, and to make it more real and powerful.

If we give without thought of reward we may discover that life sometimes returns to us far more. And when we give what is most vibrant and enduring in us, we make the world suddenly come alive for another. This is the way the world and our lives in it are transfigured. To be vulnerable to the world, which means entering into the experience of another without violation, requires uncommon integrity, courage, and gentleness.

If Chopin's music conveys anything, it conveys this sense of vulnerability, this risking of tenderness, of reaching out. The power of such human self-transcendence is vivid and direct not only in Chopin's music but also in the poetry of Shakespeare. _____ and _____ will now read to each other

from one of his sonnets. This reading, with us as witnesses, will constitute their vows to love one another, to grow in their love, and through it to reach out afresh to the world.

BRIDE   *Let me not to the marriage of true minds*
             Admit impediments. Love is not love
             Which alters when it alteration finds,
             Or bends with the remover to remove:

GROOM   *O no! it is an ever-fixed mark,*
             That looks on tempests, and is never shaken;
             It is the star to every wandering bark,
             Whose worth's unknown, although his height be taken.

BRIDE   *Love's not Time's fool, though rosy lips and cheeks*
Within his bending sickle's compass come;
Love alters not with his brief hours and weeks,
But bears it out even to the edge of doom.

GROOM   *If this be error, and upon me proved,*
I never writ, nor no man ever loved.

[*Sonnet CXVI*]

OFFICIANT   [*To the couple*] _____ , _____ , you have vowed your love to each other. Are you now ready to confirm that love in the responsibilities of marriage?

BRIDE AND GROOM   Yes.

[*Bride and groom now exchange rings and kiss. If there is a recessional, portions of the third movement from Chopin's Concerto No. 1 would provide a joyous musical conclusion.*]

1745445

symbolsandmeanings

Written by Angus Cameron for the marriage of Carl and Charlotte Marzani on November 2, 1966, this ceremony is historically oriented. The orginal appropriate function of witnesses and officiant is clearly spelled out, as well as the ancient philosophical origins of the exchange of rings and the inherent religious quality of any ceremony in which two people commit themselves indefinitely to each other. The giving and receiving of rings survives from the groom's presentation of a gift of value to his bride; in accepting it, the bride gained a measure of economic independence and dignity. By the seventh century the ring had replaced a still older gift of money or other articles of value. The custom of the gift of a single ring from the groom to the bride embodied the bias of male superiority, of activity on the part of the man and acquiesence on the part of the woman. The increasingly common practice of a double-ring ceremony indicates, therefore, an ethical movement from patriarchal to mutual and more democratically participatory concepts. In any event the giving of rings attests to the unequivocal seriousness of the intention to become committed to one another.

OFFICIANT "Dearly Beloved" is a phrase truly meaningful on these loving occasions, but especially so today in this particular company that _____ and _____ have chosen as witnesses to their vows. And so, Dearly Beloved, we are gathered here to join this woman and this man in marriage. In the dim and ancient past of their forebears this company would have been sufficient to sanctify their marriage. Indeed, in their hearts this company is sufficient now to do this, although a larger company of their fellows, in its symbolic presence, has already done so according to its proper forms. _____ and _____ have chosen to ask us, with me as your representative, to give this occasion yet another sanction.

This rite between woman and man is more ancient than the state of religion; indeed, in its natural sense, the permanent pairing of female and male is more ancient than even man himself. But surely the function, if not all the forms of marriage, is a religious one; for any occasion that calls upon a woman and a man to confront and consider their chiefest human function is a religious one in the ultimate sense. We know of no other word to describe the awe and wonder with which we face this, one of the four most meaningful occasions in man's life experience. Birth, the attainment of womanhood and manhood, marriage, and death are the four. Only two of these, the middle two, are commonly celebrated with conscious knowledge of the celebrants and only one of these, marriage, with the full and mature conscious knowledge of the celebrants. But marriage is the occasion when the fullest consciousness of woman and man makes a crucial and mutual decision. And all men at all times have considered this as a notable incident not only in the private life of the parties but in the larger life of humanity—a private decision, to be sure, but one to be celebrated before witnesses.

Our forebears required nothing more than the statement of intention of the parties before the assembly of the tribe. That the rite is a private one has been decently preserved in the very rituals of the communities from which our dear friends have sprung. The Jewish religion does not require the presence of a rabbi, as anyone may marry a couple, and the only further requirement is the presence of two witnesses, decent surrogates of the tribe itself. Indeed, the wise men of the Jewish tradition consider that in the absence of two such witnesses, then Heaven and Earth, those two bountiful elements of our natural environment, may serve as those two witnesses.

In the Roman tradition, in its most ancient past, and in the Christian tradition, the same is the case. A man and a woman marry themselves and the priest or minister serves only as the witness for his God and his church.

Their lives are their own, yet they are inseparably bound to other lives, first to those of their parents, and then to their brothers and sisters and other relatives and friends. In ancient Rome the *paterfamilias* gave the bride in marriage, as the father has done and now does in many cultures. And in deference to those ways it is fitting that the father of the bride should serve here as a special witness to these rites and by his presence take notice for all her family of the passage of the daughter to her own household.

So _____ and _____ have asked us to serve as the witnesses to their marriage—a marriage that they themselves make today. Their vows are their own and they have been spoken in their hearts before they will be spoken before us as witnesses here.

[*To the couple*] Have you, _____ , and have you, _____ , made such vows to each other, and do you call upon this company to be witnesses to those vows?

BRIDE AND GROOM   We have and we do.

OFFICIANT   [*To the wedding party*] _____ and _____ have wished to exchange these rings as symbols of their vows. And in many

40

ways this is fitting, not only because the ring is an ancient symbol of such vows, but because for another ancient tradition the circle was considered to be the perfect form of all forms in nature. The Greeks attributed such mystical qualities of perfection to the circle that when they discovered that this perfect form in its dimensional relationship produced an irrational number, they concealed this fact. Yet the Greeks knew that perfection implied imperfection; the rational, the irrational. Just so the perfect marriage symbolized by the circle of the ring must always contain the imperfection of the parties to that marriage, since the parties to it are only human. Montaigne said that if only one instruction were given at the marriage ceremony, it might be to admonish the bride and groom that successful marriage involves the avoidance of the unforgivable.

[*To the bride*] Will you, then, _____ , as you put the ring on the hand of _____ , repeat after me as the representative of these witnesses to your vows: "Behold, _____ , thou are consecrated to me as my husband, from this day forward to love and to cherish, to have and to hold, for richer and for poorer, for better and for worse, in sickness and in health so long as we both shall live."

[*To the groom*] And will you, _____ , as you put the ring on the hand of _____ , repeat after me as the representative of these witnesses to your vows: "Behold, _____ , thou art consecrated to me as my wife, from this day forward to love and to cherish, to have and to hold, for richer and for poorer, for better and for worse, in sickness and in health so long as we both shall live."

[*To the couple*] And so, _____ and _____ , in so doing and in expressing your private vows before this loving company, you have pronounced yourselves husband and wife.

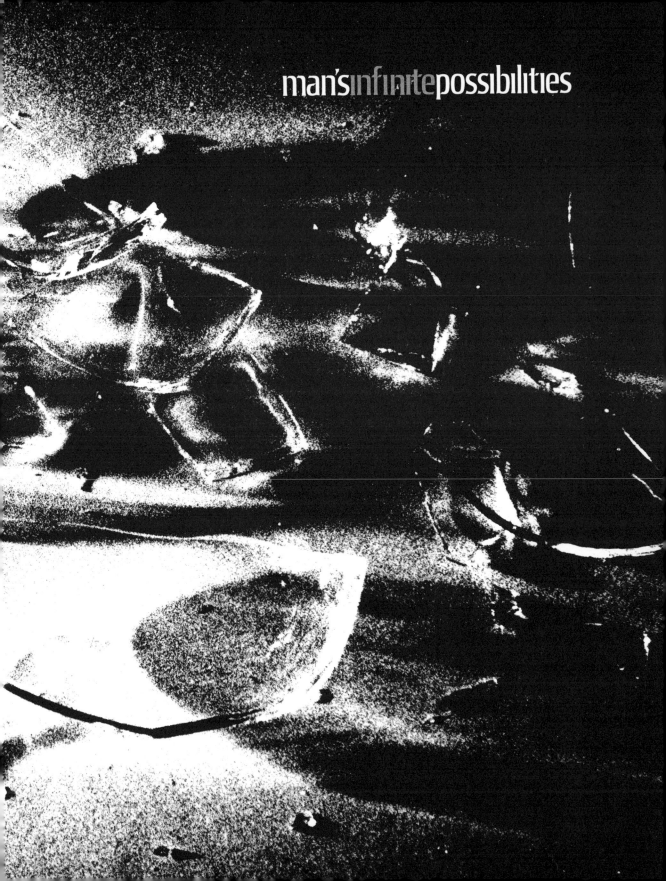

man'sinfinitepossibilities

*t*he following exuberant and cerebral ceremony is somewhat startling in its use of scientific metaphors and language, and somewhat immodest in its claims. Its authors, Eliot and Sandra Ivanhoe, invented some new words to express certain nuances of feeling and perception that could not quite be captured by more conventional language. The unusual terminology had other objectives as well: to express certain sentiments in a way that only certain people in the gathered company could fully understand; to administer a concealed rebuke to older people for thinking that their particular experience of life is more pertinent than the capacity to experience; to announce a clean break with the past and mark a very new beginning indeed. Hence the crushing of the wine glass, an ancient symbol, in the midst of a startlingly contemporary, almost fantastic statement. This Jewish custom is of uncertain genesis. Clearly it conveys the harsh warning that joy is sometimes canceled by sudden grief, and that the possibility of a genuinely new future may occasionally require a clean and conscious disjunction with the past. It also announces that there is something irreplaceable and unique in the relationship between a husband and wife, that it cannot be truly shared with any third party. Another commonly accepted understanding of this tradition is found in the officiant's comment to the couple before the goblet is shattered.

I worked on the whole statement with the couple but affected its outcome only slightly. The version presented here is the original, although a few of the more exotic peculiarities of expression have been either omitted or simplified.

Prelude Music   *Consecration of the House Overture*—Ludwig van Beethoven

OFFICIANT   We join in Beethoven's consecration and reaffirm a new consecration: the union of two already infinite plurals. This marriage is the induction of two otherwise separate but infinite beings into an infinitely larger Becoming.

GROOM   There is no limit to induction. There is no limit to the inductive growth of the We. This union of apparently two creatures is itself a growing. It is a growing into growing. Today we are celebrating the enormity of the beauty of the enormity of our growth: today, tomorrow, and beyond all tense. We affirm that lovingness and livingness are themselves united in growth, as are we.

It is therefore our glorious and divine purpose to fly mountains, to sow petalscent, to kibbutz eternity, to will time, to expand with the universe, to glorify glory, to love with love. All man-made restraints to our fulfillment self-destruct before us. The serious scholarly spirit of gravity, the lack of trust which dictates unhuman rules, in fact, anything confining, is impotent before our auto-rejuvenating kinetic potential.

BRIDE   Where there is love is there trust is there limitlessness. We affirm our limitlessness. We are flamboyant fools. Together we shall mature but never age. To grow old is a contradiction. To grow is the dictum. To mature is to become younger and younger more and more gracefully. We hereby commit ourselves to a serenity more flamboyant and more foolish than the petalfall of Magnolia.

We are both in love, and we are in love with each other. To love is to live is to create is to laugh is to revel is to share is to dance is to fly is to prevail is to grow is to smile is to dream is to live.

GROOM   We mean, of course, delight. Delight is what *We* means. This is the purest double helix of our us-ness. Ultimately, all we effect in the world is immediately self-judged by its consistency with our delight. We shall make our own conventions. Essentially, what we want you to do is feel what we are saying. Being able to feel something is the only way to know it. It is one giant step even beyond empathy until the feeling becomes *you*. We have discovered this and are rediscovering it all the time. We feel what we know.

We want to create and be part of that creation. Love, of course, has always been associated with creation. However, we are not seeking to create brand new beings only—we want to help the old become new again through love and discovery, to show them, to help them remember what wonder is, and thereby renew ourselves.

BRIDE Life for us is filled with new beginnings but never can we say, "We ended there and will begin here." Rather, the mind flows from one to another without any great demarcation, absorbing and putting out new information, feeling all that is around, whether good or bad.

There is no fear so much as a perpetual feeling of expectancy; always life is pregnant with new sensations. There must be sorrow and suffering if one is going to be able to feel the good. We are not the first to say this, but again, saying is different from feeling. To have known such really deep sorrow —to feel the horror of emptiness and then to creep slowly, ever so slowly back up the mountain; to take again and again the one step backward for two forward; to feel so much on the way and hold "joy" like the Holy Grail—as a golden vision. When this quest is ended, then and only then can real joy be felt: the joy of achievement and creation of a new being. Time is there to help one become bigger and stronger to provide room for more happiness—to make the horizon and sunrise broader.

The joy of true freedom, the freedom of the spirit—we stand before you as a tribute to the spirit of joy!

GROUP We are a living maypole! We are a succah of harvest. We are a sacrament. *We* are a progeny. And here assembled are some of the forebears of our joy: our families and friends. Today is the celebration of what we already shall become. In celebration we show you the joy you have created. And through us are past creations re-created nonstop. This never-ending continuity is manifest in the spirit of sharing.

    Sharing and trust enhance and cause each other in an infinite instantaneous cycle which powers all exploits. This is of the power to which we will, the will to power, the life-force. We are opened thereby to all possibilities and we are therefore of such strength as to allow ourselves all life experiences without squeamishness. But never must we allow ourselves to un-experience. As Blake said, "The eagle never lost so much time as when he submitted to learn of the crow."

[*Officiant holds glass of chartreuse.*]

OFFICIANT May you drink always from the full, and the empty will crush beneath you. In accordance with ancient tradition, we wish that the years of your marriage be not less than the time it would take to fit these fragments together again.

[*Bride and groom drink; groom crushes the empty glass.*]

Once again, sharing and trust enhance and cause each other in an infinite instantaneous cycle which powers all exploits. Any things which enhance and cause each other in an infinite instantaneous cycle, any things which comprise an infinite pro-gress, comprise units and examples of livingness. It is as when a man who is laughing sees himself laughing. It is the trick of serendipity whereby one can create and observe the creation at exactly the same moment: instant feedback. If there could be degrees of livingness, they could be measured by how little entropy they release.

48

GROOM   We are infinite energy-generators, but this is inconceivable. Therefore are we a miracle.

A miracle stands—or flies—beyond vows. And yet within us lies a drive which functions as a mutual vow. Evolutionists call it integration, the tendency to organize or create, the tendency *against* the tendency to dissolution, the tendency *against* entropy. This vow before vows is the affirmation to be as great as is humanly impossible.

OFFICIANT   [*To the bride*] Do you, _____, affirm to be as great as is humanly impossible?

BRIDE   Yes.

OFFICIANT   [*To the groom*] Do you, _____, affirm to be as great as is humanly impossible?

GROOM   Yes.

OFFICIANT   And so have we returned to where we began, as a union of already plurals. As a symbol of this mutual infinite instantaneous cycle, this inpansion and expansion of the Nietzchean eternal recurrence, _____ and _____ will exchange rings.

[*To the couple*]_____ and_____: In expressing your private affirmations before this public company, you have pronounced yourselves husband and wife. You now face the prospect of a richer future than either of you alone could have looked forward to before. Because you have a richer future, you will also enjoy an infinitely greater present. From this moment on, go your separate ways together, remembering always to be each other's best friend.

Postlude Music   "The End"—the Beatles. From the album *Abbey Road*

"Eyes of a Child"—the Moody Blues. From the album *To Our Children's Children's Children*

49

individualitythroughfriendship

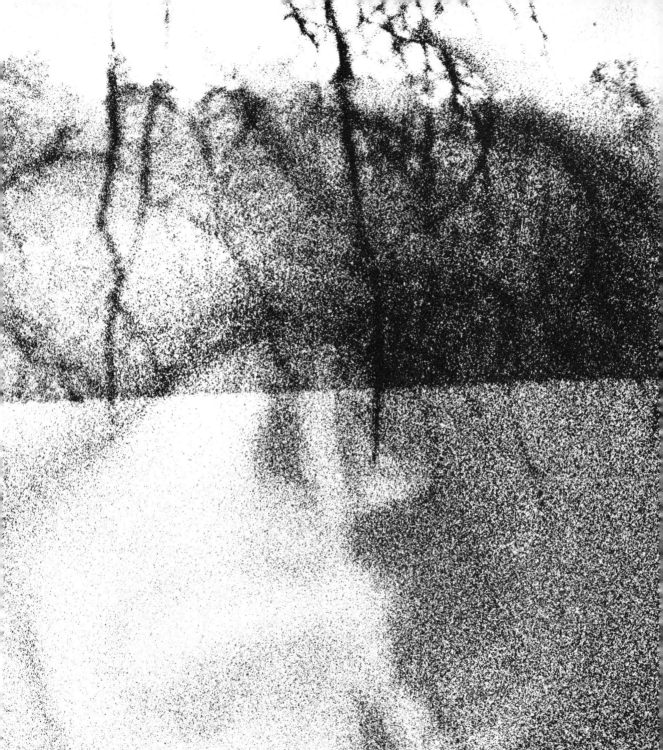

arriage ought not to be conceived of as a cure for lone-liness, as if loneliness were a disease or a misfortune. Perhaps we would be closer to the mark of the New Weddings by speaking of aloneness. Aloneness predicates the objective fact of being apart. Real friendship assumes that association be-tween different people will enhance rather than merge their distinct identities. The following ceremony dwells upon friend-ship in marriage as an outgrowth of the appreciation of alone-ness.

It was the Protestant Reformers who substituted for St. Paul's view of marriage the concept of friendship between husband and wife. This was actually a harking back to Judaic precedent (compare the Song of Solomon 5:16: "This is my beloved, and this is my friend") as well as to a medieval ideal. Inherent in the Reformers' stress on friendship in marriage was the belief that love in the form of friendship between husband and wife should actuate a marriage. This emphasis became a new dimension in marriage which has continued into our own day. The miracle of marriage, if it occurs, is that the persons party to it somehow create upon each other, which cannot occur unless the individuality of each partner continues dis-tinctively and deepens. This requires periods of aloneness, not the unending stifling togetherness so fatuously celebrated in popular songs and sermons of the 1950's.

OFFICIANT   Dear Friends, marriage, and the union it symbolizes, can be the most sublime of human experiences; for in any final accounting, love in its infinite manifestations is what life is all about. Today we come joyfully to acknowledge the decision of these two people, _____ and _____, to share their lives.

This sharing is not at the expense of each partner's individuality; rather, the uniqueness of each marriage partner is enhanced by the strength of the common bond. Marriage represents a mutual arrangement in which each is the guardian of the other's solitude. To affirm the distance between each other is to affirm the dignity of friendship in which each helps the other continually to grow, to be different, to be alone at regular intervals.

"Too often we think of love as the answer to loneliness. We put love in opposition to loneliness and think of love as an antidote to the experience of being lonely. Carson McCullers has a beautiful passage in *The Ballad of the Sad Café* in which she puts this myth to rest. Love, in fact, is a kind of loneliness, she claims. [Really to] love is always to accept the otherness, the mystery of the other, and to refuse to violate that mystery. To rape the mystery out of another person is not to love—it is tyranny."* And not only tyranny but moral self-destruction. The inability to let what is different from ourselves exist in the world is one of humankind's perennial tragedies, for which we often try to compensate by substituting external power.

It is a sign of great strength, rather than weakness, to let other people be and not interfere with the choices they wish to make. Normally what happens is that "our feelings are hurt and so we manufacture a kind of concern which is, in reality, a determination that our way will be the way of everyone. But such relationships are not only national [and inter-

---

*Quoted material in this and the following three paragraphs is taken from a sermon, "The No in Love," preached by Al Carmines of the Judson Memorial Church in New York City on March 14, 1971.

national]—they are also personal." And our chief focus here is necessarily on the personal.

Very likely, then, "the highest type of sophistication is love, namely the ability to let that which is different exist and be itself. True, that means an inevitable loneliness—but the loneliness of love is far to be preferred to the togetherness of blandness and characterlessness. Loneliness is not only a burden; it is also a privilege and a profoundly human one.

"To experience one's aloneness is to experience who one is. It is a painful journey, this journey into our identity, but its rich discoveries are the discoveries of what it means to have a self and to love that self . . . real love is the ability to say no to everything that seeks to dilute love into a kind of togetherness and protect us from our solitude and violate the solitude of another."

OFFICIANT [*To the groom*]_____, as you place your ring on _____'s finger, repeat, from the Song of Solomon, chapter 5, verse 16: "This is my beloved and this is my friend."

GROOM "This is my beloved and this is my friend."

OFFICIANT [*To the bride*] _____, as you place your ring on_____'s finger, repeat: "This is my beloved and this is my friend."

BRIDE "This is my beloved and this is my friend."

OFFICIANT Goethe wrote: "True friendship manifests itself denying at the right time, and love will often grant a harmful good when it needs more the will of the demanding one than his well-being."

It is the creative, not the indulgent, love which refines our selfishness, deepens our personalities, and makes life more meaningful.

_____ and _____, by exchanging vows and rings, you have underscored your marriage to each other in the presence of this company. From here on each of you will see your own experience in a new light as your life together unfolds. May you have the courage to love in each other and, by implication, in others on this earth, the truth that is yet to be, the truth that shall always be new.

anewhome

*t*he New Wedding often represents a break, sometimes sharp, with a person's family and their religion. This usually implies as well a rupture with the social conventions which adhere to the religion. At this juncture a minister can be especially useful to a young couple, for he can ease their families' confusion or disturbance by helping the parents comprehend the moral necessity for their children, now grown, to make their own different and radical way. The following ceremony emphasizes the distinction hereafter to be made between old family ties and the establishment of a new home. Toward this end the guests are directly addressed by the minister at the ceremony's formal conclusion.

When a couple invites guests, they are saying in effect that they want others, whether these people approve or not, to know of their choice of a life together. The invited relatives and friends have the potential responsibility to support the couple emotionally in the vows they make publicly. A wedding ceremony is another way of announcing to the world that two people are about to enter upon a special relationship which will help redefine the expectations of other men and women toward them in other relationships. Old family ties are now dissolved except those of affection; the husband and wife are henceforth to be treated as married and not single by friends and acquaintances. The wedding the couple perform does not join them; only they can do that through awareness of the bond already existing between them; the ceremony merely proclaims that fact.

OFFICIANT   Dearly Beloved, we are assembled to celebrate the joining of this man, _____, and this woman, _____, in marriage, which is to be held in honor among all men. Let us therefore remember that marriage has been established and sanctified for the welfare and happiness of mankind. It has been declared that a man shall leave his father and mother and cleave unto his wife. Those who enter this relation are to cherish a mutual esteem and love; to bear with each other's infirmities and weaknesses; to comfort each other in sickness, trouble, and sorrow; in honesty and industry to provide for each other, and for their household, in temporal things; to encourage each other in the things which pertain to the spirit; and to live together as heirs of the grace of life.

In the timeless words of the Song of Songs:

Bind me as a seal upon thine arm,
As a seal upon thy heart;
For love is as strong as death,
Mightier than the grave;
The darts of love are darts of fire,
Furious flames;
Many waters cannot quench love,
Nor floods devour it.

And in Hosea:

And I shall betroth thee unto me forever,
Yea, I will betroth thee unto me in righteousness,
And in loving kindness and in compassion;
And I shall betroth thee unto me in faithfulness.

What have each of you to say to us?

GROOM   I want to marry this woman.

BRIDE   I want to marry this man.

59

OFFICIANT [*To the couple*] You, _____, and you, _____, have now freely given voice to your desire to be united in marriage. What vows do you bring to this occasion?

GROOM [*To the bride*] I, _____, take you, _____, to be my wedded wife, to have and to hold from this day forward, for better, for worse, in plenty and in want, in sickness and in health, to love and to cherish, so long as we both shall love.

BRIDE [*To the groom*] I, _____, take you, _____, to be my wedded husband, to have and to hold from this day forward, for better, for worse, in plenty and in want, in sickness and in health, to love and to cherish, so long as we both shall love.

GROOM [*To the bride*] I give you this ring in token and pledge of our abiding affection for each other.

BRIDE [*To the groom*] I give you this ring in token and pledge of our abiding affection for each other.

OFFICIANT And may these words ever be inscribed upon the tablets of your hearts and upon your lips:

Grow old along with me!
The best is yet to be,
The last of life for which the first was made.

Inasmuch as you have accepted the vows which bind you together in your love, and by the giving and receiving of rings, have pledged yourselves each to the other in the presence of this company, I do now declare that you are husband and wife.

[*Extemporized concluding remarks*]

It is a long-established tradition that the officiant of a marriage has the privilege, if he chooses, of adding some personal comments relevant to the occasion and to the people who have come to make it a special one.

What marriage is all about is what life is all about—growth, in qualitative and ethical terms. The relationship between two people must keep growing, changing: forming a constant adventure and development which will not be without conflict. If differences are openly faced, the possibility of learning how to convert problems into opportunities will not be lost, and the marriage will prosper. A conjugal relationship may be compared to a performance of jazz, in which the crucial test for the musician is to make his mistakes mean something. May the same be true of _____ and _____ as you continually share in each other's confrontation with reality. And may you be energetic on one another's behalf, even as each of you remains ambitious for your own development.

In religious traditions that place a heavy emphasis upon ties within families and ties between families, the public aspect of marriage may seem overwhelmingly important. But let us never forget that marriage is even more a private matter between two independent human beings, a relationship upon which no one should presume to intrude without invitation or an otherwise pressingly good reason.

We have witnessed this evening a humanist commitment openly acknowledged. _____ and _____, in being wedded to each other under humanist auspices, have by their freely chosen action surmounted barriers of religious provincialism.

Marriage has always connoted not the breaking of old family ties but their transformation. Different, more mature relationships have now to be forged anew between the grown offspring who have married and their parents. The essence of the religious life is how well you live, not what creeds you profess or what rituals, liturgical or social, you observe. As the great religions at their best have recognized, it is to this moral factor that we should be most loyal. _____ and _____ have elected not to live together according to the religious loyalties of their separate families but to mark a new path with values congenial to their own view of the world.

The prerequisite for personal growth is self-transcendence. By this I mean the ability to exercise a certain detachment from events, from people, from our own preoccupations, from our own material possessions. It is all too easy to conceive of marriage as exclusively the time to start a savings account, to buy a house, to become, in short, predictable and tame. Such attitudes are in themselves not bad; but if adopted with a view toward making ourselves like everyone else, they serve only as extensions of the morally fatuous illusion that love means possessiveness, that love is fulfilled through possessing a spouse and children as well as a number of material things. Precisely because the temptation is greatest at the moment of marriage to be more and more like others must that temptation be resisted. Many a marriage is subverted by the wedding ceremony, which is why this ceremony has been different.

We may prize material possessions and social status, but it is wise not to be possessed by these belongings. They are only one of several means to the good life, while the creative life needs them hardly at all. People should no more be a function of their real estate and security holdings than they should be a function of other people's religions, thoughts, or opinions.

To make contact with the roots of your being is to act out of what you are. If that is the beginning of existential pain, it is also the beginning of sanity and authentic existence. If our basic values are humanistic, then lesser values can never dictate to us. To love well is not to dominate but to give of ourselves. The real evidence of love, whatever its manifestations, is to treat a person in his full humanness. As in all things, a delicate balance needs to be struck. William Ellery Channing, in reflecting on the essence of moral integrity, once put it this way in *My Symphony*:

To live content with small means: to seek elegance rather than luxury and refinement rather than fashion, to be worthy, not respectable and wealthy, not rich.

[*To the couple*] _____ and _____, the excitement of a marriage, as with any relationship, lies in its directness and immediacy. Here we become riveted to reality. Fidelity means staying close to reality and growing ever as a result. To love is to respond outwardly toward others from the reality of your inner life. So may you learn to give each other as many opportunities to respond as possible.

As you grow a little each day, loving many things in common and not merely each other, you will assure your future in terms that matter most. This is the first day of the rest of your life together. We trust that you will find the second day even more rewarding.

[*Officiant motions to bride and groom to turn and face the company.*]

Ladies and gentlemen, it is my pleasure to present Mr. and Mrs. _____.

growthtogether

In this ceremony, John and Sue Haefner's vows are a bit unusual in that they stress not each other's growth but the need for an understanding communication between the newly married couple. The basic tone is set by the opening statement written by Louis and Margaret Miele. Another feature of this wedding, found explicitly in no other ceremony in the collection, is parental recognition and blessing upon the union.

OFFICIANT [*To the wedding party*] _____ and _____ have honored us by inviting us to be with them during this time that will make them husband and wife.

What they mean to each other is obvious in their lives but not easily expressed in the language of a ceremony.

They are adult.

They have known each other for more than two years.

They choose to live together.

The choice is responsible, free, independent, and happy.

To convey the sense of what they wish to mean to each other, they have requested their good friend, _____, to read from I Corinthians 13.

[*Couple join hands.*]

FRIEND If I speak with the eloquence of men and of angels, but have no love, I become no more than blaring brass or crashing cymbal. If I have the gift of foretelling the future and hold in my mind . . . all human knowledge . . . and if I also have that absolute faith which can move mountains, but have no love, I amount to nothing. . . .

This love of which I speak is slow to lose patience—it looks for a way of being constructive. It is not possessive: it is neither anxious to impose nor does it cherish inflated ideas of its own importance.

Love has good manners and does not pursue selfish advantage. It is not touchy. It does not keep account of evil or gloat over the wickedness of other people. On the contrary, it is glad. . . . when truth prevails.

Love knows no limit to its endurance, no end to its trust, no dashing of its hope; it can outlast anything. It is, in fact, the one thing that still stands when all else has fallen.
[*Phillips translation of the New Testament*]

OFFICIANT [*To the couple*] Of all the men and women you know, you have chosen each other as partners in your life's journey together. Are you ready to be married?

BRIDE AND GROOM We are.

OFFICIANT   They have spoken their wish.

[*To the parents*] Will you, their parents, grant them your blessings and pledge them your love and acceptance? [*Parents may be either standing some feet behind the couple or seated in the front row.*]

PARENTS   We will.

OFFICIANT   [*To the groom*] Do you, _____ , take _____ to be your wife, to love and respect in your days together.

GROOM   I do.

OFFICIANT   [*To the bride*] Do you, _____ , take _____ to be your husband, to love and respect in your days together?

BRIDE   I do.

[*Turning toward each other, bride and groom exchange rings, then face guests and utter their vows.*]

GROOM   With this exchange of rings we want to express to family and friends our shared hope to continue exploring the exchange we have come to love over the years.

BRIDE   We will spend increasing amounts of our energy in the effort to watch and reach out for each other through good and bad times and through that reserve which seems to isolate people from one another most of the time.

OFFICIANT   In the presence of this company _____ and _____ have consented together in wedlock and have pledged themselves to each other. May they now go their ways together as husband and wife.

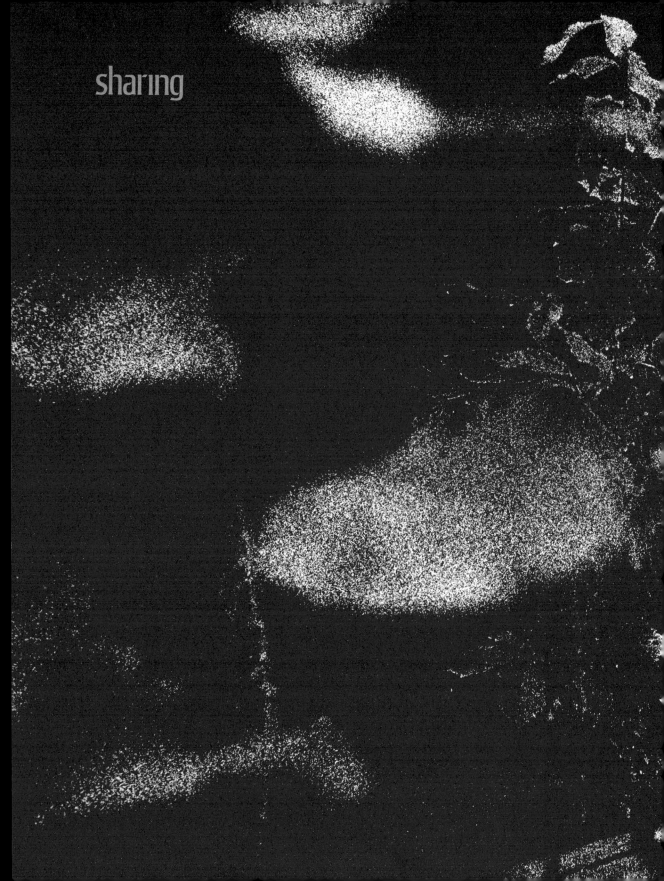

sharing

*t*his is the only one of the new humanistic ceremonies presented here which projects specifically into the future in terms of home, the procreation of children, and the sharing in old age of accumulated values.

More and more couples nowadays consciously elect to have a childless marriage in order to obtain more leisure for developing their own potential and enjoying their own pleasures. They prefer this to serving instrumentally toward the future of children. Indeed, societies of all kinds have officially regulated sex relations largely for the purpose of ensuring their future survival through the offspring of marriage; that is why children of so-called unlawful unions have faced severe legal difficulties.

No doubt the proper context for marriage is the mutual anticipation of a common future. What does giving oneself to another imply if not movement toward a future—beginning with the wedding—when relationships between two people will assume additional dimensions? One of these normally expected dimensions has been the procreation of children.

Marriage without children would have been incomprehensible to the ancient Hebrews, whose religion postulated an invisible deity manifested in nature and history. For the Jews, man was made in the image of God, but God could not be represented by sterile graven images. God therefore had to be begotten in the image of man: the faces of God were without limit in number or variety. Yahweh was a god of perpetual change and liveliness; there was a bit of God in every man. The divine image would be diminished without perpetual re-creation. Hence the injunction to multiply and replenish the earth. The so-called Seven Benedictions, recited during the traditional Jewish ceremony, try to bring the married state into dynamic relationship with creation itself and with Israel's Messianic expectations. Wedded life was a sacred trust and obligation.

Though marriage was clearly a central requirement and responsibility for the Jews because children were its inevitable and holy fruit, this obligation no longer holds today. Economic and religious demands are greatly lessened. If marriage is becoming a freer and more individual choice, so is the decision to have children or not. Only those who want children should have them; it does not follow that only those who want children should get married. Even the new Lutheran wedding service, published for trial use in mid-June, 1972, has omitted its traditional prayer for offspring in the recognition that marriage is principally the relationship between two adults.

Just as unhappiness in marriage is the consequence when one or both partners forget who they are and want to be, so also does unhappiness follow when parents forget that their devotion to each other must precede devotion to either children or society. Otherwise an emotional imbalance is created at the very center of wedded life. An undeserved burden falls on the children, and life for everyone becomes joyless as all efforts are exerted for the benefit of an impersonal future.

This particular ceremony, paraphrased from one composed by Shayne Weir (Ph.D.), offers an ethical humanist view of the relationship between children and parents within the context of a rich family life. It is interesting to note that not until as late as the Protestant Reformation was a healthy home life actually hailed as a desirable state of affairs for all people, clerical and lay. Character and destiny, it slowly came to be recognized, are fundamentally molded by the home, not by the dogmatic inculcation of theological propositions.

OFFICIANT [*To the couple*] Dear _____ and _____ . Today you are surrounded by your friends and family, all of whom are gathered to witness your marriage and to share in the joy of this occasion which should be one of the most memorable and happy days of your life.

Life has no singular meaning so much as it is composed of many meaningful events some of which can be specified and planned for. One of these events is marriage.

As you know, no minister, no priest, no rabbi, no public official, can marry you. Only you can marry yourselves. By a mutual commitment to love each other, to work toward creating an atmosphere of care and consideration and respect, by a willingness to face the tensions and anxieties that underlie human life, you can make your wedded life come alive.

On this the day of your marriage, you stand somewhat apart from all other human beings. You stand within the charmed circle of your love; and this is as it should be. But love is not meant to be the possession of two people alone. Rather it should serve as a source of common energy, as a form in which you find the strength to live your lives with courage. From this day onward you must come closer together than ever before, you must love one another in sickness and in health, for better and for worse, but at the same time your love should give you the strength to stand apart, to seek out your unique destinies, to make your special contribution to the world which is always part of us and more than us.

Today, as you join yourselves in marriage, there is a vast and unknown future stretching out before you. The possibilities and potentials of your married life are great; and now falls upon your shoulders the task of choosing values and making real the moral dreams that other men and women have engendered and died for. In this way, you will create the meaning of your life. If your love is vital, it will make the choosing and acting easier for you.

In traditional religions it is customary to call down a blessing upon the bride and groom. But I know that you share with me the conviction that how two people love and treat one another and contribute to the community of men and women is more important than their formal religious beliefs. You stand before me today as two mature and thoughtful people who wish to express their emotions within the framework of a meaningful life. For your self-reliance and courage and love, you deserve respect, and it is these attributes which make this a serious but not solemn occasion.

I should like at this time to try to speak of some of the things which many of us wish for you. First of all, we wish for you a love that makes both of you better people, that continues to give you joy and zest for living, that provides you with energy to face the responsibilities of life.

We wish for you a home—not a place of stone and wood, but an island of sanity and serenity in a frenzied world. We hope that this home is not just a place of private joy and re-treat, but rather serves as a temple wherein the values of your life are generated and upheld. We hope that your home stands as a symbol of humans living together in love and peace, seek-ing truth and demanding social justice. We hope that your home encompasses the beauty of nature—that it has within it the elements of simplicity, exuberance, beauty, silence, color, and a concordance with the rhythms of life. We wish for you a home with books and poetry and music—a home with all the things which represent the highest strivings of men and wo-men.

We wish for you children—children who will not be mere reflections of yourselves but will learn from you your best traits and will go forth to re-create the values you shall have instilled in them. We hope that you will give your children the freedom to find their own way, that you will stand by them when they need you and will stand aside when it is time for them to seek their personal destinies. But we hope you will pass on to your children the concept of family, not as an eco-nomic unit but as a transcendent force which brings people close in time of joy and in time of need.

Finally, we wish that at the end of your lives you will be able to say these two things to each other: Because you have loved me, you have given me faith in myself; and because I have seen the good in you, I have received from you a faith in humanity.

[*To the groom*] _____ , please place this ring on _____ 's finger. Do you, _____ , promise _____ that from this day onward she will be your wife and you will stand with her in sickness and health, in joy and sorrow, and do you pledge to her your respect and your love?

GROOM   I do.

OFFICIANT   [*To the bride*] _____ , please place this ring on _____ 's finger. Do you, _____ , promise _____ that from this day onward he will be your husband and you will stand with him in sickness and health, in joy and sorrow, and do you pledge to him your respect and your love?

BRIDE   I do.

OFFICIANT   Now, according to the form of solemnization of marriage by the state of _____ , but most of all by the power of your own love, I pronounce you married. You may now call yourselves by those two old and respected names: husband and wife.

thewineofthespirit

Nothing in the law requires an exchange of rings in a marriage ceremony. In this instance the force of custom reveals itself as more powerful than the force of law. It is rare, even in a New Wedding, to omit rings altogether. The distinguishing negative feature of the following ceremony, however, is that it does dispense with rings. The New Wedding, after all, is protean rather than procrustean. The distinguishing positive feature of this ceremony, apart from the fact that it explores the relation between love and justice, is the prominence of the pouring and drinking of wine. Wine has ever been the symbol of life and earth. Here it is also referred to as a sign of the hope that time carries, the change that time promises—but only if we take the initiative in using time, in becoming historical agents on our own behalf: in breaking the cup. Indeed, a further refinement in the ceremony itself might be to have the bride and groom crush their own cups. The omission of rings in this context can be regarded as a political act of nonparticipation: the refusal to submit to conventional capitalist expectations. But this inference, among others, is better left to the imagination; a wedding should not be an exercise in polemics.

OFFICIANT Dear Friends, marriage allows two people to grow and redefine themselves as individuals and as lovers. It succeeds only
to the degree that each partner respects the individual other—
when each, becoming part of the other and a part of the marriage, does not slip into the shadow of the beloved.

Just as one partner cannot lose himself in the other, so a
couple cannot use marriage as an escape from the world.
Two people must accept their responsibility as part of the human community. Their love may make it easier to carry their
responsibility but cannot be a means to avoid it.

We who are friends and relatives of _____ and _____
share with them on this wedding day of theirs some of the
same convictions. Especially do we take note of the special
relationship between love and justice.

Perhaps "the most pernicious myth about love is the image
of love as a closed system between two people, or three people,
or one man and his country, his religion, his race, his family.
However, the sweet intimacy of love inevitably turns rancid
when it circles in upon itself and is not open to the whole
world. For love is finally a way of being with the world. In
the world there are those whom we are naturally closer to and
drawn to—but the love that is real is not the exclusive property of [celebrities] enclosed in some cinema paradise. For
the true love is a prism through which one loves the whole
world. Every intimacy and every sweetness of love makes
the whole world different and opens one up to the world's
reality rather than protecting one from it. That is why love
must always say no to the sly seduction . . . to love in a closed
world with just the perfume of the beloved and no other smells
from nature or humanity."*

Kahlil Gibran writes in *The Prophet*—

*From Al Carmines' sermon delivered on March 14, 1971, at the Judson Memorial
Church, New York City.

81

Love one another, but make not a bond of love:
Let it rather be a moving sea between the shores of your
*   souls.*
Fill each other's cup but drink not from one cup.

[*To the couple*] _____ and _____, in consonance with
Gibran's sentiment, would you now drink to one another?
Fill each other's cup, but drink from your own. Let this act
signalize your promise to one another to be yourselves and to
risk what you are for the sake of what you yet can be.

Let this drinking of wine remind you that what matters most
in life is the spirit, not the letter; the wine, not the cup. The
future is forever in the making, so do not cling too long to any
present, however satisfying, lest it become an anchor and
therefore a dead past rather than a springboard and therefore
a usable past.

[*Bride and groom are handed two chalices. Each in turn pours*
wine from the same bottle into the other's cup.]

May your days and years to come be filled with the integrity and joy that will enable you to abide through all times
of ambivalence and doubt. And if your affection for each other
has always a little more to grow, it will rise from you and enter
the lives of others, enriching and strengthening them. As Saint-
Exupéry puts it: "Love does not consist in gazing into each
other's eyes, but in looking together in the same direction."

BRIDE AND GROOM   *We shall not cease from exploration*
And the end of all our exploring
Will be to arrive where we started
And know the place for the first time.
[T. S. Eliot, Four Quartets]

OFFICIANT   In making public this bond uniting them, _____ and _____
are now husband and wife.

spiritualfreedom

matrimony is a legal institution, but that is no reason to assume that the order consequently demanded by law necessarily interferes with the real freedom of a marriage. The following ceremony stresses the great spiritual freedom which the individual parties can import into their private lawful relationship. Being concerned for another, yet learning when to leave another alone —one of marriage's perpetual challenges —is implicit in the vows of this ceremony. Though modest, the vows are unconditional and contain the explicit recognition of rational risk and of the unpredictable adventure of growth and development together.

"Till death do us part" is still the central vow in many conventional ceremonies. It derives from the old Catholic dogma of the indissolubility of the marital bond. But is it not clearly absurd to attach divine absolutism to the imperfect possibilities of human choice? Love is what sanctifies a marriage and endows it with whatever moral texture it evolves.

One of the minor Swiss Protestant Reformers was Bucer, who would permit a married couple to divorce when love had ceased to cement them. A New Wedding will characteristically enjoin the partners to take one another "from this day forth," or "so long as love shall last." Historically speaking, then, it expresses a Protestant rather than a Catholic position. The old dispensation taught that marriage had to be lifelong since it was a sacrament. The new dispensation teaches that a marriage can be lifelong only if its partners keep it growing emotionally, spiritually, morally. Fidelity is the consequence rather than the cause of spontaneous love. Marriage requires imagination and effort, and the spontaneous love which undergirds it can easily take a lifetime to disclose its abundance, novelty, and depth. In The Second Sex Simone de Beauvoir avers that fidelity is essential "because the desire felt by two people in love concerns them as individuals; they are unwilling for this to be contradicted by experiences with outsiders; they want each one to be irreplaceable for the other."

OFFICIANT We are drawn at this hour to honor and take joy in the con-
vergence of two lives, those of _____ and _____, in marriage, which is a fitting estate for the sanity, well-being, and
enrichment of mankind.

Marriage is founded upon that most enduring yet elusive of
human sentiments —love. And as E. E. Cummings reminds us:

love is more thicker than forget
more thinner than recall
more seldom than a wave is wet
more frequent than to fail

it is most mad and moonly
and less it shall unbe
than all the sea which only
is deeper than the sea

love is less always than to win
less never than alive
less bigger than the least begin
less littler than forgive

it is most sane and sunly
and more it cannot die
than all the sky which only
is higher than the sky

Marriage is also a civil ceremony. Not surprisingly, its dual
origin in law and sentiment makes it seem a curious institution.
But even so profound a skeptic as Bertrand Russell was per-
suaded that the institution was worth preserving. His words
clarify our feelings today:

It is therefore possible for a civilized man and woman to be happy
in marriage, although if this is to be the case a number of conditions
must be fulfilled. There must be a feeling of complete equality on
both sides; there must be no interference with mutual freedom; there
must be the most complete physical and mental intimacy; and there

must be a certain similarity in regard to standards of values. . . .
Given all these conditions, I believe marriage to be the best and most
important relation that can exist between two human beings.

> [Marriage and Morals]

[*To the couple.*] Will you, at this time, express to each other
the vows you have chosen?

GROOM [*To the bride*] _____ , I want to live with you just as you are.
I choose you above all others, to share my life with me, and
that is the only evidence there can be that I love you.*

I want to love you for yourself in the hope you will become
all that you can be. I promise to honor this pledge as long as
life and faith endure.

BRIDE [*To the groom*] _____ , I want to live with you just as you are.
I chose you above all others, to share my life with me, and
that is the only evidence there can be that I love you.

I want to love you for yourself in the hope you will become
all that you can be. I promise to honor this pledge as long as
life and faith endure.

OFFICIANT [*To the groom*]_____ , what pledge do you offer in token of
these vows?

[*Groom presents ring to officiant.*]

GROOM This ring.

OFFICIANT [*To the groom*] In offering this ring, which marks your desire
to enter into the days of your life together with another, repeat
after me: "With this ring I marry you and join my life with
yours."

*Adapted from Denis de Rougemont, *Love in the Western World*, New York, 1956,
page 305.

GROOM   [*To the bride*] "With this ring I marry you and join my life with yours."

OFFICIANT   [*To the bride*] _____, what pledge do you offer in token of these vows?

[*Bride presents ring to officiant.*]

BRIDE   This ring.

OFFICIANT   [*To the bride*] In offering this ring, which marks your desire to enter into the days of your life together with another, repeat after me: "With this ring I marry you and join my life with yours."

BRIDE   [*To the groom*] "With this ring I marry you and join my life with yours."

OFFICIANT   Since _____ and _____ have consented together in the bond of matrimony and have pledged themselves each to the other in the presence of these witnesses, be it thereby acknowledged that they are husband and wife.

We can derive no moral from love except the moral to love more deeply. We can expect nothing from love except what love gives. We cannot choose what chances and changes may befall us, but we can shape the spirit with which we shall meet them.

May these two people, now married, in accepting the affection of friends and relatives here present, try to return their love to the world, remembering, in the words of Kahlil Gibran:

But if in your fear you would seek only love's peace and love's pleasure,
Then it is better for you that you cover your nakedness and pass out of love's threshing-floor,
Into the seasonless world where you shall laugh, but not all of your laughter, and weep, but not all of your tears.
    [The Prophet]

Thus may the love of _____ and _____ for each other, and which they feel for the rest of you, grow stronger and richer, and their marriage be fruitful.

ananarchist-feminist wedding

*t*his ceremony is as much an overt political statement, inspired by anarchist thought and the Women's Liberation Movement, as it is a mutual expression of personal commitment. Tensions between the individual and the state are honestly presented and resolved for practical purposes.

It may appear that those who originally composed this New Wedding make unnecessarily heavy weather out of the state's legal presence in any form. The form at issue here is the marriage license, the public requirement for which was first passed in England in 1753. Actually that requirement is far less stifling than the injunctions which any religious licensing body might impose. The purpose of issuing licenses is to ensure records for the fiscal, legal, and census-taking authorities. The state does not in actuality interfere with the spirit, scope, or novelty of any marriage. Its goal is to regulate at a distance, not to impose positive content. Nonetheless, in view of the citizen-surveillance activities of modern government, any information-gathering becomes suspect, because data originally sought for record-keeping can easily be used for repressive objectives. So this ceremony's protest against the symbolism of the state as a licensing authority needs to be seen in the light of recent history.

An unsuspected irony in the ceremony is that it uses a single ring, which historically denotes male superiority over the female. However, this wedding remains an eloquent and uncompromising expression of the principle that the more independent each partner is in marriage, the freer each becomes to love the other. As freedom grows, dullness and mediocrity of response diminish.

thenewwedding

Introduction   "Glenn Gould Plays Bach," Partita #1, Columbia D3S754

OFFICIANT   We are gathered together here as relatives and friends of _____ and _____ . They have honored us by choosing us to witness their public testament of marriage, which will make them husband and wife.

BRIDE'S FATHER
When, in disgrace with fortune and men's eyes,
I all alone beweep my outcast state,
And trouble deaf heaven with my bootless cries,
And look upon myself, and curse my fate,
Wishing me like to one more rich in hope,
Featur'd like him, like him with friends possess'd
Desiring this man's art, and that man's scope,
With what I most enjoy contented least;
Yet in these thoughts myself almost despising,
Haply I think on thee—and then my state,
Like to the lark at break of day arising
From sullen earth, sings hymns at heaven's gate:
    For thy sweet love remember'd such wealth brings
    That then I scorn to change my state with kings.
    [*Sonnet XXIX, Shakespeare*]

BRIDE   We love each other, but we do not want to get married except for reasons of prudence. We do not want to get married because we do not regard the state as having the authority to regulate and define our relationship to each other. Unless we come together solely upon our own authority, we cannot take full responsibility for our love for each other, as we wish to do. Our feelings about human love and state authority are well expressed by the nineteenth-century anarchist Michael Bakunin:

We are convinced that in abolishing . . . civil and juridical marriage, we restore life, reality, and morality to natural marriage based solely upon human respect and the freedom of two persons: a man and a

96

woman who love each other. We are convinced that in recognizing the power of either party to the marriage to part from the other whenever he or she wishes to, without having to ask anyone's permission for it — and that likewise in denying the necessity of needing any permission to unite in marriage, and rejecting in general the interference of any authority with that union — we make them more closely united to each other.*

GROOM   We reject not only the authority of the state over us, we also reject the traditional and legal authority of man over woman, which has no legitimate moral basis. We wish you to understand that we do not love each other any less for rejecting these two traditional authorities, but rather, on the contrary, that it is *because* we love each other that we try to resist them. Now we find it prudent, however, despite these deeply held beliefs, to bind ourselves together in marriage.

OFFICIANT   [*To the bride*] _____, will you have this man to be your wedded husband, to share your life with him, and do you pledge that you will love, honor, and care for him in tenderness and affection through all the varying experiences of your lives?

BRIDE   I will.

OFFICIANT   [*To the groom*] _____, will you have this woman to be your wedded wife, to share your life with her, and do you pledge that you will love, honor, and tenderly care for her through all the varying experiences of your lives?

GROOM   I will.

OFFICIANT   [*To the groom*] _____, do you offer _____ a token of this marriage?

*The Political Philosophy of Bakunin, P. Maximoff, editor, Glen Cove, New York, 1953, page 236.

GROOM   Yes. _____, as a token of our love, I place this ring on your finger.

[*While groom places the ring on bride's finger, the officiant pours two glasses of champagne before them.*]

OFFICIANT   May the bride and groom now drink a mutual toast.

[*Bride and groom retain their glasses after silently toasting one another.*]

Inasmuch as _____ and _____ have consented together in this ceremony to live in wedlock and have stated their vows before these witnesses, and before me, as representative of the community, I call upon all here to recognize that they are now husband and wife.

   To _____ and _____, may I extend my best wishes for your continued happiness, today and the days of your lives. May I ask you both to abide in your dedication, as expressed by the prophet Micah, to "do justice and love mercy," and walk with empathy and compassion the paths upon which you will accompany your fellow men and women now, and in the future.

[*Music: "Canzon Septimi," Toni No. 2, Giovanni Gabrieli, Columbia MS 7209*]

I propose we all now toast the bride and groom.

[*Groom moves to fill glasses.*]

I propose a toast to the bride and groom.

Afterword *Research done by the bride and groom who created this ceremony revealed that the anarchist wedding has a long tradition
in history.**

    *When Robert Dale Owen (son of Utopian Robert Owen)
married Mary Jane Robinson in 1832, he said in part:*

*Of the unjust rights which in virtue of this ceremony an iniquitous
law tacitly gives me over the person and property of another, I cannot legally, but I can morally, divest myself. And I hereby distinctly
and emphatically declare that I consider myself, and earnestly desire to be considered by others, as utterly divested, now and during
the rest of my life, of any such rights, the barbarous relics of a feudal,
despotic system.*

*When Lucy Stone married Henry Blackwell in 1855, the two
joined hands and read a long statement, including the following:*

*While we acknowledge our mutual affection by publicly assuming
the relationship of husband and wife . . . we deem it a duty to declare that this act on our part implies no sanction of, nor promise
of voluntary obedience to such of the present laws of marriage as
refuse to recognize the wife as an independent, rational being, while
they confer upon the husband an injurious and unnatural superiority.*

    *The bride in the anarchist-feminist wedding tried vigorously
to retain her own name, despite official recognition of the
marriage. She had the legal option to pay the $125 fee required
to change her married name back to her maiden name but
refused to do so. Some states require a name change, many do
not; taking the husband's name is deemed a privilege and is
not mandatory. No legal action is necessary for a woman to
retain her name at marriage—so long as she does not start
using her husband's name in the first place. A woman can peti-
tion to change her name back, but it takes time and money.*

*The two ceremonies mentioned below can be found in Up *from the Pedestal, Aileen
Kraditor, editor, Chicago, 1968.*

99

Legal complexities can be considerable. Credit cards, for example, are not issued to a woman in her maiden name without legal proof of a name change. Most states consider marriage a matter of "intent" even though no certificate is taken out.

All this may seem so much bother about nothing, but it is not. For the tradition of the woman dropping her own name and assuming that of her husband is part and parcel of the tradition that regarded women as men's property. Wives were supposed to give up their past and become one flesh and one name with their husbands. Again, the hidden assumption is that the husband provides the woman with her identity, since she is expected to submerge whatever of her own she has acquired. The spirit of the New Wedding does not insist that the bride keep her maiden name, because the willingness to counter the cultural biases and legal hassles must be an individual decision. Still, it is necessary that we understand the psychology behind the name change in marriage. A New

Wedding must embody the recognition that a real marriage represents a coming together of two independent equals who choose to share common interests, goals, aspirations; it is not expected that such a choice will entail a denial of either partner's past. Therefore if a bride feels particularly sensitive about the name change, she should feel free to retain her maiden name.

It is a growing conviction among some that the state should recognize every marriage contract so long as there is adequate provision for wife and children. That is, the state should simply legalize any reasonable agreement between spouses. The contract might include a husband's advance consent to his wife for an abortion, as well as agreements on the splitting of income, on the effort and time each partner will devote to housework and child care, and on sexual rights and liberties. In short, the new sexual equalitarianism demands that a bill of particular expectations and responsibilities be drawn up along with any New Wedding ceremony. To counter the argument that this approach makes matters rationalistically cut and dried, those in favor of a contract point out that creating one is a valuable learning process which may uncover hitherto unknown differences and conflicts: the more knowledge, the more intelligent the love.

But the contractual approach may also be an indication of insecurity: of an inability to face and deal with unknown factors as they turn up, and of an unwillingness to trust oneself and another. Completely to foreclose risk in a love relationship is to foreclose love itself.

reachingout

*t*his wedding was originally composed for my own marriage. I have changed it periodically, so that what is reproduced here is quite different from the original although its basic structure remains. A wedding should have the following aspects in roughly this order: a welcome to the guests, a few observations (and/or quotations) about life, love, marriage, society; the vows and exchange of rings, and a proclamation that matrimony is the result of the ceremony. The vows can either precede the final words by the officiant or serve as the logical consummation of the nuptial proceedings.

The Western wedding ceremony has consisted of two elements: the espousals and the betrothals. With the onset of the Middle Ages the espousals, originally secular, and separate in time from the betrothals, were a private, informal expression of the intention to become husband and wife. Eventually this private exchange was made sacred by a priestly blessing at the door of the church. Then followed the intrinsically religious ceremony of the marriage vows, the nuptials: this was the betrothal. Only with subsequent consummation of sexual intercourse did the union become technically indissoluble and the marriage an irrevocable sacrament. In early Western folk customs unmistakable evidence of the bride's defloration had to be offered sometime during the wedding festivities. Those who have seen the film Ryan's Daughter will recall this occurrence during the Irish wedding gaieties.

OFFICIANT | Dear Friends, we are gathered here at this hour to witness and to celebrate the drawing together of two separate lives. We have come so that this man, _____, and this woman, _____, may be joined in marriage. It is not to be entered into lightly but with certainty, with mutual respect, and with a sense of reverence which does not preclude beauty, humor, or joy.

Love can be one of the highest experiences that comes to humankind. At its best it reduces our selfishness, deepens our personalities, and makes life far more meaningful.

All significant experiences are of concern to our fellow men and women. Two people in love do not live in isolation from the wider embraces of humanity. To achieve love is not to be absolved of social responsibility. So it is that the institution of marriage is ordained as a public recognition of the private experience of love and as a sanctifying of both parties to its greatest purposes.

Matrimony symbolizes the ultimate intimacy between a man and a woman; yet this closeness should not diminish but strengthen the individuality of each partner. A marriage that lasts is one that always has a little more to grow. The poet Rainer Maria Rilke once said that marriage is not a matter "of creating a quick community of spirit by tearing down and destroying all boundaries, but rather a good marriage is that in which each appoints the other guardian of his solitude. . . . once the realization is accepted that even between the closest human beings infinite distances continue to exist, a wonderful living side by side can grow up, if they succeed in loving the distance between them" no less than one another.

Kahlil Gibran echoed these sentiments in *The Prophet:*

*Sing and dance together and be joyous, but let each one of
    you be alone,
Even as the strings of a lute are alone though they quiver
    with the same music. . . .
And stand together yet not too near together:*

For the pillars of the temple stand apart,
And the oak tree and the cypress grow not in each other's
shadow.

Thus it is out of the resonance between individuality and union that love, whose incredible strength is equal only to its incredible fragility, is born and reborn.

Today's celebration of human affection is therefore the outward sign of a sacred and inward commitment which religious societies may consecrate and states may legalize, but which neither can create or annul. Such union can only be created by loving purpose, be maintained by abiding will, and be renewed by human feelings and intentions. In this spirit these two persons stand before us.

Will you now please clasp your right hands?

[*To the groom*] Do you, _____, take _____ to be the wife of your days, to love and to cherish, to honor and to comfort, in sorrow or in joy, in hardship or in ease, to have and to hold from this day forth?

GROOM I do.

OFFICIANT [*To the bride*] Do you, _____, take _____ to be the husband of your days, to love and to cherish, to honor and to comfort, in sorrow or in joy, in hardship or in ease, to have and to hold from this day forth?

BRIDE I do.

OFFICIANT [*To the groom*]_____, what pledge do you offer in token of these vows?

[*Best man hands the ring to the groom who, presenting it to the officiant, answers, or the groom may present it himself.*]

107

GROOM   This ring.

OFFICIANT   [*To the groom*] As you place this ring, symbol of your commitment in marriage, on the third finger of _____'s left hand,
repeat after me: With this ring I wed you and pledge my faithful love.

GROOM   [*To the bride*] With this ring I wed you and pledge my faithful
love.

OFFICIANT   [*To the bride*] _____, what pledge do you offer in token of
these vows?

[*Maid of honor hands the ring to the bride who, presenting it
to the officiant, answers, or the bride may present it herself.*]

BRIDE   This ring.

OFFICIANT   [*To the bride*] As you place this ring, symbol of your commitment in marriage, on the third finger of _____'s left hand,
repeat after me: With this ring I wed you and pledge my faithful love.

BRIDE   [*To the groom*] With this ring I wed you and pledge my faithful love.

OFFICIANT   Forasmuch as _____ and _____ have consented together
in wedlock, and have pledged themselves each to the other in
the presence of this company [*or*, these witnesses], I do now
pronouce that they are husband and wife. Let all others
honor their decision and the threshold of their house.

For one human being to love another: that is perhaps the hardest of
all our tasks [says Rilke again], the ultimate test and proof, the
work for which all other work is but preparation. . . . Love . . . is a
high inducement to the individual to ripen, to become something in

himself, to become . . . [a] world to himself for another's sake, . . . [human love] consists in this, that two solitudes protect and touch and greet each other.*

May these two people, now married, fulfill this covenant which they have made. May they openly give and take from each other, encouraging each other in whatever trials that may befall them, sharing in each other's joys, helping each other as each occasion requires. Having grown to trust themselves and each other, may they be unafraid to trust and welcome life. Yet may they not merely accept and give affection between themselves but also seek the lonely and the outcast in friendship. May they be willing and grateful to return love.

We who are present, and those not here who care, hope that the inspiration of this hour will not be forgotten. May they ever seek to achieve the perspective of serenity amidst conflict and of courage amidst any twilight of despair. Novelist George Eliot once asked: "What greater thing is there for two human souls than to feel that they are joined . . . to strengthen each other . . . [and] to be one with each other in silent unspeakable memories."

*Rainer Maria Rilke, *Letters to a Young Poet,* translated by M. D. Herter, Norton, New York, 1934, pages 53, 54, 60.

companionsforlife

*t*he following ceremony, which in a way is an alternative
to the preceding one, indicates an already great maturity and
a prescient understanding that even a lifetime is not long
enough for the love between two people to disclose its abundance. Its authors are Robert and Susan Okin.

OFFICIANT Friends, we are gathered here at this hour to witness and to celebrate the coming together of two separate lives. We have come to join this man, _____, and this woman, _____, in marriage, to be with them and rejoice with them in the making of this important commitment. The essence of this commitment is the taking of another person in his or her entirety, as lover, companion, and friend. It is therefore a decision which is not to be entered into lightly, but rather undertaken with great consideration and respect for both the other person and oneself.

Love is one of the highest experiences that we human beings can have, and it can add depth of meaning to our lives. The sensual part of love is one of life's greatest joys, and when this is combined with real friendship both are infinitely enhanced. The day-to-day companionship—the pleasure in doing things together, or in doing separate things but in delighting to exchange experiences—is a continuous and central part of what a man and a woman who love each other can share.

Marriage symbolizes the intimate sharing of two lives, yet this sharing must not diminish but enhance the individuality of each partner. A marriage that lasts is one which is continually developing and in which each person is individually developing, while growing in understanding of the other. Deep knowledge of another is not something that can be achieved in a short time, and real understanding of the other's feelings can develop fully only with years of intimacy. This wonderful knowledge of another person grows out of really caring for the other so much that one wants to understand as completely as possible what the other is feeling. Thus it is possible to share not only joys and successes but also the burden of sorrows and failures. To be known in this way is a priceless thing, because such understanding and acceptance make it easier to live with our problems and failings and worries. But, again, while marriage is the intimate sharing of two lives, it can yet enhance the differences and individuality of each partner. We must give ourselves in love, but we must not give ourselves away. A good and balanced relationship is one in which neither person is overpowered or absorbed by the other. Thus it is out of the tension between separateness and union that love, whose incredible strength is equal only to its incredible fragility, is born and reborn.

We are here today, then, to celebrate the love which _____ and _____ have for each other, and to give social recognition to their decision to accept each other totally and permanently. Into this state of marriage these two persons come now to be united.

GROOM   [*To the bride*]_____, I take you as my wife. I pledge to share my life openly with you, to speak the truth to you in love; I promise to honor and tenderly care for you, to cherish and encourage your own fulfillment as an individual through all the changes of our lives.

BRIDE   [*To the groom*]_____ , I take you as my husband. I pledge to share my life openly with you, to speak the truth to you in love; I promise to honor and tenderly care for you, to cherish and encourage your own fulfillment as an individual through all the changes of our lives.

OFFICIANT   Since_____ and _____ have vowed to be loyal and loving toward each other, formalizing in our presence the existence of the bond between them, we bear witness to the ceremony they have performed—the ceremony that has made them husband and wife.

[*Musical Interlude: Bach, "Adagio for Strings"*]

May these two people, now married, keep this covenant which they have made. May they be a blessing and a comfort to each other, sharers of each other's joys, consolers in each other's sorrows, helpers to each other in all the vicissitudes of life. May they encourage each other in whatever they set out to achieve. May they, trusting each other, trust life and not be afraid. Yet may they not only accept and give affection between themselves, but also together have affection and consideration for others.

We who are here present, and those who are absent thinking of these two people, hope that the inspiration of this hour will not be forgotten. May they continue to love one another forever.

customsandtraditions

Old customs often continue imperfectly—that is, in diluted, disguised, or upgraded form—even though they are obsolete: for example, the custom of the father presenting the bride. The giving away of the bride is a Protestant heritage. In Roman Catholic and Jewish weddings the father escorts but does not give away his daughter. Although historical accuracy is hard to achieve where myths and legends are abundantly interspersed with facts, the historical freight attached to wedding customs is immense. It can be very helpful to know something of what is behind certain customs in order to feel free to use, reinterpret, or omit them in the pursuit of our own objectives.

Customs are usages, habits, practices that express and regulate social life. They not only possess immediate pertinence but also symbolize complex and enduring nuances. All customs were originally new, an obvious truth we seldom realize. Take, for instance, the increasing practice of living together before marriage. As we noted earlier, this fact is being publicly admitted in some of the new ceremonies as one of the significant events leading to marriage. But how can it be symbolized in the wedding, whether or not it is specifically mentioned in the ceremony? More often than not such a fact is a matter of common knowledge.

The Arrival of the Bride and Groom — A bride and groom who have been living together may elect to enter the scene together without benefit of parental or other escort; or, reversing the usual drama entirely, they may choose to be on the scene from the beginning and greet their friends as they arrive. If the couple have not been living together, it is symbolically precise for them to enter from separate locations at the time the ceremony is scheduled to start. All these procedures are alternatives to the ritual in which the bridegroom waits for his bride to be delivered to him by the proud father, with the mother beaming her approval from the front row.

If one or both partners were previously married and have children still to be raised, the couple can be preceded by the children. It is in keeping with the spirit of the New Wedding if any older children wish to say a personal word of welcome upon the occasion of the coming together of the families.

The Wedding Dress
One of the litanies of marriage folklore counsels the bride to wear "something old and something new, something borrowed and something blue." The idea is that her wedding garments should symbolize continuity with her family past (something old and borrowed), and express her own uniqueness (something new and blue). Blue came to signify the innocence and freshness of first love; it thus refers to the outgoing aspect of affection for another and is apparently older than the idea of bridal white.

Not until the mid-nineteenth century did special wedding dresses, and white in particular, become obligatory. Before then even the well-to-do regarded it as unjustified extravagance to buy a garment for one day's use only. Brides simply wore the best dress they had, with perhaps a special touch of blue.

Even when they first became popular, white wedding dresses were simple, not the gratuitously ornate and expensive items that a consumer-oriented culture was eventually to insist upon. At her own wedding Queen Victoria wore a simple white silk gown with matching veiled bonnet. But by the end of that increasingly comfortable era named after her, a growing middle class that aspired to common amenities had made expensive white wedding clothes virtually compulsory. Much absorbed with the purity and sexual innocence of women, the Victorians apparently borrowed the idea of bridal white from the virgin-white outfits little girls put on for their first Communions.

The Veil   The bride's veil and bouquet are of greater antiquity than her white dress. The veil, which was yellow in ancient Greece and red in ancient Rome, and which usually shrouded her from head to foot, has since early times connoted the subordination of woman to man. In the modern era, of course, the veil became white in order to accompany the dress. The thicker the veil, the more traditional the implication of wearing it.

According to tradition, on their wedding day it is bad luck for the bride to be seen by the groom before the ceremony. Indeed, in the old days of marriage by purchase they hardly saw each other at all, courtship being a very recent historical emergence. The Anglo-Saxons expected brides to hide their faces completely within their long tresses. In short, the ancient wedding was designed to be a surprise for both bride and groom; as to how pleasant or unpleasant this experience was we can only imagine. In any event, when the husband lifts the veil at the end of the ceremony he symbolizes male dominance. If the bride takes the initiative in lifting it and thereby presents herself to him, she is showing more independence. The New Wedding will have nothing to do with veils or with anything else that constitutes socially approved concealment or coquetry.

The Bride's Bouquet   The bride's bouquet seems to have started with sprigs of orange blossoms. These were carried by the Saracens during their wedding rites as a symbol of fertility, and subsequently as more abstract emblems of happiness and good luck. The Saracen custom was brought to Europe by the returning Crusaders. The Roman bride had carried ears of wheat (later changed to corn) so that her husband's grain bins would always be full. By the time of the Renaissance, whatever stalks were carried by the bride were reduced to a sheaf; by the eighteenth century, a bouquet of flowers had become the practice, and so it remains when it is followed.

Sometime in the last two centuries, tossing the bridal bouquet came to serve as a substitute for the rough and unseemly scramble for the bride's garter. Tradition has it that if an unmarried young woman happens to catch the bouquet, she herself will be married soon.

Rice and Petals Throwing rice and confetti, or releasing a shower of flower petals, originally symbolized the hope for fertility in marriage. Today rice and flower petals bear more generalized wishes for beauty, happiness, and prosperity, as do many ancient customs in their simplified contemporary versions. For a New Wedding the use of flowers is preferable to rice, because children may not be the couple's main objective.

Bride-Prices and Money and marriage have been interwoven almost from the
Dowries beginning. Prior to this inevitable material relationship was marriage by capture. The tepid modern survival of that crude method of obtaining a spouse is the groom's custom of carrying his bride over the threshold. Also, the "best man," who stands to the groom's right during the ceremony and does little more than hold the bride's ring for him, was in the dim past the friend who helped the groom abduct the woman he wanted. This was outright theft, and the men in the woman's family would go off in hot pursuit. Meanwhile the groom sequestered himself and his stolen spouse in a hideout; they kept out of view for awhile. The modern-day honeymoon emerged from this exciting, dangerous practice. So did mock-resistance rituals in certain cultures, ceremonies in which the woman goes through the physical motions of not wanting to get married and thereby increases the ardor of the husband-to-be. Except as ritual, the use of force eventually gave way to primitive business arrangements: marriage by purchase.

In ancient Israel, and in old England, for instance, a man's daughter represented an investment. Her status was directly

proportional to the price she could fetch from a potential suitor. Since his daughter was his property, the father would literally sell her off to the highest bidder, although we can assume that humane considerations played a part in many transactions. (The symbolic survival of this well-known custom occurs in traditional wedding ceremonies when the father is asked to give his daughter to the man about to marry her.)

A suitor might pay for a wife by turning over some property to the father or by working for him for a stated period. The father would set the amount of the purchase; in time, as civilization became mobile, money served as an acceptable substitute for either property or labor. The cost of purchasing a wife was known as the bride-price, which was turned over to the bride's parents as a gift. Much later the bride-price became a gift for the bride, to enable her to cover unforeseen contingencies in marriage. A simple ring for the bride was sometimes an affectionate external sign that the bride-price had been fully paid—although, as we are aware, many other meanings have become attached to the ring over the centuries, such as the notion of unbroken union. It was not uncommon practice in ancient times for men to seal a pact or contract with a ring, and surely marriage has entailed both those aspects. The kiss at the end of the marriage ceremony, of course, subsequently became a personal sealing of the pledges just made.

We may speculate that the custom of the bride-price represented a static social order in which all the cards were stacked in favor of a patriarchy which young men could not enter without overcoming numerous obstacles. Sometimes exasperation would set in if demands were too high, and the bride-price might be obviated by the woman's agreement to run away with her suitor. This was the origin of the elopement.

The dowry developed as a kind of balancing factor, a way of compensating the groom for his newly assumed burden of supporting a woman. Paying the parents for a wife thus disappeared as the privileges of male chauvinism were extended to other men besides the tribal elders. (The equivalent of that sum, however, might be given instead to the bride by the groom in the form of a marriage gift. But the dowry remained; even in our own time young girls may put away certain goods, like sheets or tableware, in their "hope chests" as the beginning of a dowry, to which their families may add, in anticipation of a wedding day.)

A dowry made a young woman more marriageable, and a father's prestige depended on his marrying off his daughter at the appropriate time. The woman simply passed from the tyranny of one household, benevolent or brutal, to that of another.

The dowry has usually consisted of the money, estate, or property a woman brings to her husband in marriage. Though it is shareable with her husband, in some societies the dowry has also been looked upon as a way of ensuring the woman's independence if she outlives him, or if she is divorced or abandoned. For example, though a woman was a handmaiden to her husband in ancient Israel, she enjoyed a position superior to that of her Greek counterpart, for she was regarded as a person with legally recognized rights to her own property. In traditional Jewish law a husband would put his obligations to his future wife in writing before the ceremony, thereby enabling her to receive a certain portion of his estate in case he died or divorced her. The idea was to prevent her from becoming a liability to the husband's family.

For the most part the tradition of the formal dowry is waning; it is coming to be admitted that the most precious thing one can bring to a marriage is oneself. Love should actuate a marriage, not the prospect of goods.

The Matchmaker For centuries the matchmaker has enjoyed an honored if occasionally ridiculed function. Groups that wanted to ensure ethnic identity regularly employed the services of a matchmaker, whose commission was a certain percentage of the dowry. Today the data-processing machine has to some extent succeeded to this delicate office. Computers can allegedly match individual backgrounds and traits so accurately that two people brought together for a date will have a pleasant time. For, say, $10, a person can receive a minimum of five contacts for potential dates; results are even guaranteed, although they are not specified! In any event, only dating is arranged, not marriage. So matchmaking of a sort has not disappeared; it has merely changed its appearance and emphasis, as is the case with any custom that expresses enduring human needs.

Eastern Rites We have concentrated largely on Western marriage; wedding rites in the Eastern churches are a separate, exotic affair laden with mystical implications and perfumed with incense. The explicit verbal content is theologically orthodox and largely alien to people not closely associated with that richly traditional community. During the long wedding ceremony, it is interesting to observe, both man and woman are crowned, the purpose being to dramatize the fact that each must reign in his or her own sphere in the kingdom of the home, and share appropriately in the joys and tribulations of married life.

Traditional Trembles   In one of his novels John Updike refers to "the white tremble of the ceremony." As a matter of fact, conventional wedding preparations are always something of an ordeal, as most people who have gone through them will agree. By the time of the ceremony vast efforts have been channeled into the event. Bride, groom, and everyone else involved in the preparations are so excited and exhausted that Updike's phrase is an apt description of what the presiding clergyman commonly sees.

In contrast, the emotional keynote of the New Wedding is joy and a sense of expansiveness, not a sense of relief that everything will soon be over. In this happy spirit most people, including the bride and groom, dress differently for the ceremony; few are trembling in white. Indeed, some wedding parties display a magnificent informality, dazzling splashes of color, and exuberant individuality in the clothes that are worn. It is all testimony to the expansion of personal freedoms in our time. Let us hope this indicates that the inner and the outer person are closer together than ever before.

sacramentandcontract

Whereas for the Jews, marriage was designed for perpetuation of the race and enhancement of the divine image, for the early Christians it was an abomination which was avoided by the pure in heart. Indeed, in the New Testament an altogether startling notion of marriage was set forth: its purpose was not the procreation of children, let alone the personal sexual fulfillment of husband and wife, but the prevention of fornication. The Old Testament had forbidden not fornication but adultery, since as a man's property a wife was not to be defiled. But St. Paul went further to proclaim the wife's obligation to be obedient, the sinfulness of divorce, and the usefulness of marriage as a way to dampen and restrain lustful appetites: "it is better to marry than to burn" (1 Corinthians 7:9). Husband and wife were to be "one flesh," a concept that has not been contravened until late in our own day.

Although New Testament teaching did not assert the superiority of the celibate over the marital state, Paul's influence was in that direction. As a multifaceted genius he was ambiguous in his approach, since for him marriage was an imperfect metaphor for the mystical union of Christ and the Church. Virginity came to be regarded as a special offering by the soul to Christ as spouse. Virginity and monasticism, which attached the concept of isolation to that of purity, grew in approved status in the early Christian community. Although the ultimate meaning of the theological doctrine of the Incarnation was to sanctify human life, the antiphysical bias of early Christianity was notable. The whole idea was to dignify life not in a spatiotemporal frame but in terms of eternity. The Incarnation, the divine intrusion of timelessness into time, carried the implication that whenever the eternal channels could be opened up, human life became capable of redemption from its grosser aspects.

The Romans There is no doubt that in attributing souls to outcasts, sinners, slaves, and women, Christianity democratically placed everyone, whatever his earthly estate, within the circle of salvation. The status of women in the Roman world was greatly elevated as a consequence. Though still "one flesh" with their husbands, they at least had the cultural sanction to choose a religious vocation instead of continuing a marriage. Nonetheless, the Romans were nonplussed by the early Christian community's lack of interest in the family and by its obsession with unworldly innocence. Certainly they did not appreciate the claim that isolated religious devotion was superior to concern for daily affairs.

Roman marital laws dealt not with the individual but with households are represented by their head, the *paterfamilias*. Love in the sense of romantic passion was regarded as a trifle and ruled out of the marital domain. The purpose of marriage was to produce children who would worship the household deities and serve the state. An authoritarian state characteristically encourages the unwavering loyalty it believes is engendered by a strong patriarchal family system. Yet the Roman wedding itself was replete with animal sacrifices and lusty joyous feasting, as if such abandon were the couple's last fling before they prudently shouldered familial responsibility.

Marriage in Rome was a private contract that could be initiated or terminated with little formality, but the levels and styles of marriage were elaborately worked out for different social classes. Emperor Justinian later took the position, different from the usual Roman attitude, that marriage, being based on love, should be dissoluble by mutual consent if love ceases. Not until the Reformation would such an opinion be heard again.

Development in the Christian Church As the early centuries went by, the Christian community began to realize that Christ's second coming would not be in the near future and that they must settle down to running their daily lives in a realistic if pious manner. They reluctantly recognized marriage as the inevitable source of social stability, although they considered individual happiness and fulfillment on earth to be incidental to the hard work of creating a Christian home in a Christian cosmos. At first the Church ignored the formality of marriage. Weddings consisted of simple rites—mostly vows—uttered by the groom: "I take you," or "Be thou consecrated to me." Bit by bit, the Church intruded itself upon the ceremony by performing a primitively officiating role in which the partners were informally required to pledge observance of the terms of the contract before witnesses.

Christianity confirmed and extended the idea of monogamy but coupled it with the duty of faithfulness, which eventually rendered the union indissoluble. With St. Augustine, marriage began to be seen less as a contract and more as a sacrament, and therefore as a vehicle of divine grace. Nonetheless, civil marriages remained common during the early centuries; ecclesiastical sanction emerged much later as the Church became dominant over the state. The indissolubility of marriage did not become firmly established dogma until about A.D. 900, and not until the eleventh century did marriage take its place as one of the seven Catholic sacraments.

In sum: The classical Catholic view came to be that marriage is not essentially a legally binding contract but a solemn, unconditional covenant under God executed in the presence of representatives (the couple's friends and relatives) of the universal Christian family. The goal of marriage is to beget the children of God and thereby sanctify human existence.

Despite the Catholic insistence upon the absoluteness of the religious bond, the notion of contract in marriage was never obliterated. Marriage implies consent and consent implies contract. This entails the recognition, if not of two equals, then of two individuals. Thus throughout the greater part of its historical development, marriage has contained an aspect, sometimes small, sometimes large, of free choice. A contract, with its implicit realistic attitude of forbearance, of give-and-take, stands against absolutist inclinations; it preserves the potential for freedom and individuality. Even at the center of the Roman Catholic tradition, bride and groom are ministers of the sacrament of matrimony; they become vehicles of grace by virtue of their religious motivation, whose sincerity actuates the ritual. The officiating priest is merely the first among witnesses; he provides the ecclesiastical blessing but does not himself perform the sacrament.

One may suppose that this view is in keeping with the popular illusion that marriages are somehow made in heaven: therefore, since man did not establish marriage, he cannot annul it by means of his laws. It follows logically, but not empirically, that marriage is founded in nature and that death alone can dissolve the union between husband and wife—assuming, of course, that each was a baptized believer to begin with. (Mixed marriages with unbelievers—heretics, Jews and pagans—were discouraged.) We can understand why divorce had to be forbidden in order to preclude the embarrassment of meeting more than one spouse in the afterlife.

The Protestant Reformation
Western Europe lived under canon law until the Protestant Reformation, which returned marriage to its Roman civil origins. In breaking the Roman Church's profitable monopolistic manipulation of the sacraments, among which was matrimony, Luther and Calvin indicated the growing claims of the national state. Comparatively lenient on divorce, the Reformers rejected marriage as a sacrament and refuted the position that death alone could dissolve it. In doing so they opened the way for a more individualized approach to both marriage and divorce. Divorce from an adulterous partner of either sex became allowable, and the offended spouse was permitted to remarry. We should not forget that the Reformation in England virtually started with Henry VIII's insistence upon obtaining a divorce from Catherine of Aragon.

Striking back in order to regain authority, the Catholics

decreed at the Council of Trent in 1563 that no marriage would be considered valid unless presided over by a parish priest in the presence of two or more witnesses.

The French Revolution

For the most part, matrimony remained a religious (a Protestant or Catholic) affair in Europe until the French Revolution, at which time the state assumed the power to validate marriages through the presence of a secular officer. Liberal divorce laws were enacted in France in September, 1792. Revolutionary doctrine proclaimed that the ease of obtaining a divorce was a necessary inference of the individual's right to freely choose his own destiny. Clearly, the authority to validate a marriage had long been a power game between church and state. Normally, as we have already observed, a religious ceremony in Europe today cannot be executed prior to the civil marriage. In the United States the civil and religious ceremonies occur simultaneously.

The Puritans

The Reformers introduced the concept of friendship in marriage between husband and wife; they also reevaluated the home and gave it a position above that of monastic isolation. This went directly counter to the Pauline view.

The English Puritans, however, partially canceled the Reformers' attitude: the common religious allegiance of a marriage was deemed more important than the couple's mutual concern for each other's cares and development. Loyalty to God was regarded as superseding all other loyalties within marriage or without. This is what gave the Puritans their enormous drive and energy to remake the world; personal pleasure was subordinated to common tasks. Nonetheless, the reconceived Protestant emphasis on friendship in marriage remained a fixed expectation and proved to be a useful one on the rugged frontiers of the New World. Marriage, for the Puritans, was of public concern and common to all mankind.

It was inevitable that in time the secularizing momentum of Western culture would overtake marriage. Part of that momentum was the modern romantic impulse in literature and the arts that became evident in the last century. Though late in flowering, the roots of this individualistic ideal can be traced back to the troubadours, who idealized passion, or romantic love. This love, the purpose of which was individual happiness and ecstasy, was attainable only outside marriage, because by the time of the troubadours in the twelfth century, marriage itself had become virtually platonized. The ideal marriage was considered to be a sort of continent cohabitation. Since sex was in such ecclesiastical disrepute, the only allowable sentiment a man could direct at a respectable woman had to be unattainable. With unsatisfied desire at its core, love could be beautiful only if platonic. The whole Western marriage tradition has been riven by this tension between passion and fidelity: Can passionate love exist within marriage? If not, where does one look for it? Does fidelity sterilize passion? Does passion destroy fidelity?

The New Wedding   The New Wedding has no truck with these artificial dichotomies and does not seek answers to them. The emotional and intellectual movement in today's New Wedding is a profound return to and reconception of the historic ideas embodied in marriage: the old idea of *sacrament* (although without the implication of permanent, indissoluble union), for whenever two people commit themselves indefinitely to each other, a religious situation is created; the old idea of *contract* (and today that tends to be spelled out in considerable detail); the old idea of *friendship*, but interpreted today as the rejection of the merging of one partner's personality with the other's. Institutionalism is played down, for in a sense these three ideas heretically extended in our day, are tied together in the spirit of Thomas Paine's liberating assertion that our own inner universe, our own mind and heart, is our real church.

134

proseandpoetry

ove poetry abounds throughout the ages, but much of it is self-consciously passionate or sentimental. Excessive passion or sentimentality are equal distortions of love and reality. All the poetry incorporated in the ceremonies described earlier was deliberately chosen to reinforce the humanistic premises of the New Wedding.

To take an example, the love poetry of the sixteenth-century English poet Edmund Spenser is not used here because, like the troubadours, he speaks of unrequited love for unattainable ladies. Indeed, Spenser's combination of Platonism and Puritanism takes us into a fantastic realm far from directness and reality. For similar reasons we avoid the poetry of Spenser's contemporary, Sir Philip Sidney. Though his amatory verses can be delightful, they are full of the pastoral symbolism of the Bible.

In contrast, a poet like Shakespeare has a formidable grasp of human nature and an incredible understanding of moral values. To quote selectively from some of his lines is to underscore the candor and psychological realism from which the New Wedding draws its strength.

Thus so far as we are concerned, poetry with a timely or timeless ring is preferable to quotations featuring Biblical pastoral imagery. Such a world is no longer with us, and to invoke it is to return nostalgically to a period that has no discernible dynamic relevance to our own. There is a difference between going back for its own sake, and going back to pick up a significant lost thread in order to carry it forward anew.

Again, perspective and discrimination are needed. To quote a simple, timeless marriage vow from the Old Testament Song of Songs ("This is my beloved and this is my friend") is one thing; it is quite another to quote from the same source such dated sentiments as "the smell of thy garments is like the smell of Lebanon," or "thy hair is as a flock of goats that lie along the side of Mount Gilead."

Classical poetry is largely excluded too, for in classical statements the individual is merely representative of a larger assemblage which is deemed more real than a single person. The New Wedding is unsuited to classical views that subordinate the individual to larger unities, whether natural, social, or religious. The Catholic doctrine that marriage is founded in nature and is indissoluble, rendering human feelings secondary; the socialist conviction that marriage must subserve community needs and objectives as defined by the state—these are subversive of the individual-in-community ethos of the New Wedding.

All this is to say again that the romantic impulse is at the base of what we are considering here—though not a romantic impulse that has become twisted into a degrading obsession. The love embodied in the spirit of the New Wedding is not the oppressive agony depicted in Tolstoy's *The Kreutzer Sonata*, Zola's *Nana*, Maugham's *Of Human Bondage*, and numerous other literary expressions by male authors who can only conceive of the tyranny of sex, the enslaving potential of passion.

It need merely be mentioned that the overall setting of a marriage ceremony is what communicates its unique character. The verbal content must always be seen in relation to its *gestalt:* a too conspicuous commercial atmosphere, like the artificial chapel of a catering establishment, may dilute and diffuse the pointedness of a New Wedding, while too much physical grandeur, like a rugged Oregon beach with loudly crashing waves, will dwarf or overwhelm the ceremonial content. If such a grand setting is desired, however, then the ceremony should be planned as a visual more than an auditory experience. This brings us into the legitimate realm of theater, but such considerations are beyond the purview of this book. We merely wish to remind readers that the total unity of a wedding should be kept in mind.

prose and poetry

The same wind moves us
but not in the same way
The same earth holds us,
but not in the same place
The same sun feeds us
and we share each
other's lives, holding
each other's shadows.

[*Harvey to Karla*, Celestial Arts, *San Francisco, 1970.*]

Becoming is a lot like dying.
You leave a lot of life behind
Not so long ago
I never said no—
I said yes. I was sweet. I was kind.

Learning is a lot like forgetting
Learning to be docile
Learning to say yes—
Learning to be me
Was forgetting to be
The idea of someone else's happiness.

Loving is a lot like indifference.
When you love enough you learn to care. . . .
Love is what's real
Not just what you feel
Love is what is here and not only what is there.

I love what's like you about me
And I love in you
What's different from me.

[*From the opera* The Journey of Snow White, *quoted in a sermon preached*
by Al Carmines, Judson Memorial Church, New York City, March 14, 1971.]

139

94

being to timelessness as it's to time,
love did no more begin than love will end;
where nothing is to breathe to stroll to swim
love is the air the ocean and the land

(do lovers suffer?all divinities
proudly descending put on deathful flesh:
are lovers glad?only their smallest joy's
a universe emerging from a wish)

love is the voice under all silences,
the hope which has no opposite in fear;
the strength so strong mere force is feebleness:
the truth more first than sun more last than star
—do lovers love?why then to heaven with hell.
Whatever sages say and fools,all's well.

> [E. E. Cummings, 95 Poems,
> New York, 1958.]

Let me insist that fidelity in marriage cannot be merely that negative attitude so frequently imagined; it must be active. To be content not to deceive one's wife or husband would be an indication of indigence, not one of love. Fidelity demands far more: it wants the good of the beloved, and when it acts in behalf of that good it is creating in its own presence the neighbour. And it is by this roundabout way through the other that the self rises into being a person — beyond its own happiness. Thus as persons a married couple are a mutual creation, and to become persons is the double achievement of "active love." What denies both the individual and his natural egotism is what constructs a person. At this point faithfulness in marriage is discovered to be the law of a new life. . . .

140

A life allied with mine, for the rest of our lives—that is the miracle of marriage. Another life that wills my good as much as its own, because it is united with mine. . . .

To be in love is not necessarily to love. To be in love is a state; to love, an act. A state is suffered or undergone; but an act has to be decided upon. Now, the promise which marriage means cannot fairly be made to apply to the future of a state in which I am at the moment, but it can and should mortgage the future of conscious acts which I take on—to love, to remain faithful, to bring up my children. . . . The imperative, "Love God and thy neighbour as thyself" . . . creates structures of active relations. The imperative, "Be in love!" would be devoid of meaning; or, if it could be obeyed, would deprive a man of his freedom.

[*Denis de Rougemont,* Love in the Western World, *translated by Montgomery Belgion, New York, 1956, pages 309–311.*]

The Master Speed

No speed of wind or water rushing by
But you have speed far greater. You can climb
Back up a stream of radiance to the sky,
And back through history up the stream of time.
And you were given this swiftness, not for haste
Nor chiefly that you may go where you will,
But in the rush of everything to waste,
That you may have the power of standing still—
Off any still or moving thing you say.
Two such as you with such a master speed
Cannot be parted nor be swept away
From one another once you are agreed
That life is only life forevermore
Together wing to wing and oar to oar.

[*Robert Frost,* Complete Poems, *New York, 1949.*]

thenewwedding

Love is a thing to walk with, hand in hand,
Through the every-dayness of this workday world,
Baring its tender feet to every flint,
Yet letting not one heart-beat go astray
From beauty's law of plainness and content. . . .
Such is true love, which steals into the heart
With feet as silent as the lightsome dawn
That kisses smooth the rough brows of the dark,

And has its will through blissful gentleness, . . .
A love that gives and takes, that seeth faults, . . .
But loving-kindly ever looks them down
With the o'ercoming faith that still forgives. . . .

[*Adapted from* The Poems of
James Russell Lowell, *New York, 1896.*]

Marriage is a great institution, especially for the children.

[*Mark Twain*]

Nature has her proper interest
And he will know that it is,
*   who believes and feels,*
That everything has a life of its own,
And that we are all one life.

[*Samuel Taylor Coleridge*]

. . . love is an outgoing movement, an impulse toward another person, toward an existence separate and distinct from one's own, toward an end in view, a future. . . .

[*Simone de Beauvoir,* The Second Sex,
New York, 1953, page 472.]

True love is . . . infinite, and always like itself. . . . it is seen with white hairs and is always young in heart.

[*Honoré de Balzac. Tryon Edwards,*
C. N. Catrevas, and Jonathan Edwards (comps.),
The New Dictionary of Thoughts, *New York, 1954, page 714.*]

143

The last word is the most dangerous of infernal machines, and the husband and wife should no more fight to get it than they would struggle for the possession of a lighted bombshell.

[*Douglas Jerrold. Tryon Edwards,*
C. N. Catrevas, and Jonathan Edwards (comps.),
The New Dictionary of Thoughts, *New York, 1954, page 714.*]

But what we think is less than what we know; what we know is less than what we love; what we love is so much less than what there is. And to that precise extent we are so much less than what we are. . . .

[*R. D. Laing,* The Politics of Experience,
New York, 1967, page 14.]

Portrait: My Wife

"I'd rather be loved, and love, than be Shakespeare."
Ambition is what calls the mountain till it comes,
Or goes where it is and gnaws the mountain down.
But she is not ambitious. She makes a choice,
Which, being she, is foregoing neither wholly,
As: how should she not be of the many-parted poet
Miranda sometimes, Lear's daughter, or Elizabeth,
Or not be as she is, fresh beauty to the muse?
She writes; is a woman; Shakespeare would know her.

As for the other, loving her makes me that poet.
Once I desired her, not seeing who she was,
Having been then married to her a morning's years,
To the straight smooth back, the opening kiss,
The laughter a red peony thrown and bursting.
She is my stranger every day. She is wretched
With doubt; everyone seeks her reassurance;
Quick-tempered as firecrackers, scornful, clean;

A spiritual materialist, Eve with clothes on.
No one knows her loneliness or believes it;
Not I, but that it is the edge of my world,
And when she comes back, then I can come back
From looking over. She is warm, her cheek is warm.
Bored with sameness, we re-read one another.
We break up housekeeping to keep our house alive,
And are thought a steady pair. Oh, she has her wish!
She, whatever she does next, is my one wish.

[*John Holmes,* "The Fortune Teller"; Poems, *New York, 1961.*]

Love—is anterior to Life—
Posterior—to Death—
Initial of Creation, and
The Exponent of Earth—

[The Complete Poems of Emily Dickinson,
edited by Thomas H. Johnson, Boston, 1960.]

songsandmusic

Most commercial music played at weddings—for instance, by a single accordionist, a pianist, or a three-piece band—is an unqualified abomination. In planning their wedding very few people consider the uniqueness of the event as a criterion for determining what music is appropriate. If a couple do not have musical preferences for their wedding, or cannot get intelligent guidance in this delicate area, it is better that they have none at all. Music should be optional.

It is impossible to be anything but arbitrary in offering suggestions, since musical tastes vary so greatly. Be that as it may, here are some views that might serve as general guides for those who are interested. We are speaking of setting the mood before and after a wedding; unless carefully chosen, music interspersed throughout the ceremony is often conducive to melodrama and should be discouraged.

Quartet music, which at its best is direct, pure, and unmonumental, is a vast repository to choose from. Depending on the mood you want to establish, you can select a movement from a polished eighteenth-century quartet or use one of the powerful meditative movements from Beethoven's last quartets. Samuel Barber's "Adagio for Strings" is tense, forthright, reverential in tone. Selections from Bach's two concertos for three harpsichords can be played to create a universe of light and energy which does not overwhelm. Handel's "Water Music" imparts a sense of stateliness and certainty. Grieg's "Wedding Day at Troldhaugen" is vigorous and gay, while a haunting atmosphere can be produced by Fauré's "Requiem." "The Wedding Cantata" (with texts from the Song of Songs) by Daniel Pinkham speaks of loving affection in a fresh contemporary idiom; its dissonance is lush. Much of Chopin's piano music is reflective, direct, passionate. The second movement from Brahms' "Double Concerto for Violin and Cello" creates a strong romantic mood. A couple who want something popular which embodies theatrical vibrancy and urgency cannot do better than the wedding processional from *The Sound of Music* or "Sunrise, Sunset" from *Fiddler on the Roof.*

Flute, guitar, and lute music are appropriate, not to mention the extensive repertoire of rock. Folk music can also be moving and relevant for a New Wedding—for example, the Shaker song which contains the following lines:

'Tis the gift to be simple,
'Tis the gift to be free,
'Tis the gift to come down
Where we ought to be.

And when we find ourselves
In the place just right,
It will be in the valley
Of love and delight.

[*Particular recordings or arrangements are a matter of personal choice*]

"Amazing Grace," English hymn by John Newton (popular rock revision by Arlo Guthrie)

Bach: Brandenburg Concerto No. 2 in F (second movement)

Bach: Brandenburg Concerto No. 3 in G (first movement)

Bruch: Violin Concerto in G Minor (second movement)

Mendelssohn: Violin Concerto in E Minor (second movement)

Mozart: Andante in C for piano and flute

Rachmaninoff: "Vocalise" (instrumental version)

Schubert: Moment Musical in F Minor for piano; also various songs (e.g., "Frühlingstraum," with its sophisticated expression of both the pain and joy in love)

Stravinsky: "Symphony of the Psalms"

Telemann: Sonatas

Vaughan Williams: "Fantasia on a theme by Thomas Tallis"

Wieniawski: Violin Concerto No. 1 in F-sharp Minor ("Prayer" movement)

Wieniawski: Concerto No. 2 in D Minor (second movement)

for further reading

for those who care to puruse in depth the themes and ideas raised in each chapter, the following suggestions for further reading in books and articles constitute a selective guide.

Getting Married Today   Beauvoir, Simone de. *The Second Sex*. Translated and edited by H. M. Parshley. New York: Alfred A. Knopf, Inc., 1953.

Bowman, Henry A. *Marriage for Moderns*. With a foreword by David R. Mace. New York: McGraw-Hill, Inc., 1970.

Ellis, Havelock. *Havelock Ellis on Life and Sex: Essays of Love and Virtue*. Garden City, N.Y.: Garden City Publishing Company, Inc., 1937.

Fletcher, Joseph. *Situation Ethics: The New Morality*. Philadelphia: Westminster Press, 1966.

Francoeur, Robert T. *Eve's New Rib: Twenty Faces of Sex, Marriage, and Family*. New York: Harcourt, Brace, Jovanovich, Inc., 1972.

Friedan, Betty. *The Feminine Mystique*. New York: W. W. Norton & Company, Inc., 1963.

Fromm, Erich. *The Art of Loving*. New York: Harper & Row, 1956.

Gould, Robert E. "Some Husbands Talk about Their Liberated Wives," *New York Times Magazine*, June 18, 1972, p. 10.

Greer, Germaine. *The Female Eunuch*. New York: McGraw-Hill, Inc., 1971.

Isben, Henrik. *The Doll's House: A Play.* New York:
D. Appleton and Co., 1889. Now available in Modern
Library and Penguin editions.

Lichtenberg, Margaret Klee. "Two Can Live as Freely as
One" (Review of book, *Open Marriage: A New Life
Style for Couples* by Nena O'Neill and George
O'Neill). *The Nation*, April 24, 1972, pp. 537–539.

Lippmann, Walter. *A Preface to Morals.* New York: The
Macmillan Company, 1929.

Millett, Kate. *Sexual Politics.* Garden City, N.Y.: Doubleday & Company, Inc., 1970.

"New Marriage Styles." *Time*, March 20, 1972, pp. 56–57.

O'Neill, Nena, and George O'Neill. *Open Marriage: A New
Life Style for Couples.* New York: M. Evans and Co.,
Inc., 1972.

Otto, Herbert A. "Has Monogamy Failed?" *Saturday Review*, April 25, 1970, p. 23.

Perutz, Kathrin. *Marriage Is Hell.* New York: William
Morrow & Company, Inc., 1972.

"Pictogram: Wedding Bells for the '70's—Marriages Booming
Again," *U.S. News & World Report*, Dec. 8, 1969,
pp. 66–67.

Roy, Rustum, and Della Roy. "Is Monogamy Outdated?"
The Humanist, March/April 1970, pp. 19–26.

Schwartz, Oswald. *The Psychology of Sex.* Harmondsworth,
Middlesex: Penguin Books, Inc., 1962.

Seaman, Barbara. *Free and Female: The Sex-Life of the
Contemporary Woman.* New York: Coward, McCann
& Geoghegan, Inc., 1972.

Shaffer, Helen B. *Marriage: Changing Institution.* Editorial Research Reports, Vol II, no. 13, Oct. 6, 1971. Washington, D. C.: Congressional Quarterly, Inc., 1971.

Sheresky, Norman, and Marya Mannes. "A Radical Guide to Wedlock." *Saturday Review*, July 29, 1972, pp. 33–38.

Wadler, Joyce. *Seventeen's One Plus One: Getting Married and Beginning a Home.* Radnor, Pa.: Triangle Publications, Inc., 1972.

Walker, Brooks. *The New Immorality: A Report on Spouse-Trading, Pornography, Playboy Philosophy, and Situation Ethics.* Garden City, N.Y.: Doubleday & Company, Inc., 1968.

The Nature of the New Wedding

Black, Algernon D. *If I Marry outside My Religion.* Public Affairs Pamphlet no. 204A. New York: Public Affairs Committee, Inc., 1966.

Decter, Midge. *The New Chastity: and Other Arguments against Women's Liberation.* New York: Coward, McCann & Geoghegan, Inc., 1972.

"The Free-form Wedding Game." *Life*, Sept. 26, 1969, pp. 95–102.

"I Take Thee, Baby." *Time*, July 4, 1969, p. 57.

"A Joyful Happening." *Time*, Oct. 17, 1969, p. 66.

Krich, Aron, with Sam Blum. "Marriage and the Mystique of Romance." *Redbook*, November 1970, p. 65.

Lamont, Corliss. *A Humanist Wedding Service.* Buffalo, N.Y.: Prometheus Books, 1971.

LeShan, Eda J. *Mates and roommates: new styles in young marriages.* Public Affairs Pamphlet no. 468. New York: Public Affairs Committee, Inc., 1971.

Lindbergh, Anne Morrow. *Dearly Beloved: A Theme and Variations.* New York: Harcourt, Brace & World, Inc., 1962.

Mace, David R. *Marriage: East and West.* Garden City, N.Y.: Doubleday & Company, Inc., 1960.

Maynard, Fredelle. "New Rites for Old." *Seventeen*, March 1969, p. 154.

McCarroll, Tolbert (ed.). *Humanist Wedding Ceremonies.* Humanist Pamphlet no. 8. New York: American Humanist Association, 1964.

Moran, Mary. "The Bride Goes Barefoot: Styles of the New Weddings." *New York*, Sept. 7, 1970, pp. 36–40.

Morris, John. "Something Old, Something New . . ." *America*, Nov. 28, 1970, pp. 459–460.

"Old Country Weddings: Italian, Greek, Polish, and Danish" (with recipes). *McCall's*, June 1970, p. 96.

Perutz, Kathrin. "Marriage: Do You Promise to Like." *Mademoiselle*, May 1972, p. 202.

Reuben, David. "What's Happening to Marriage." *McCall's*, January 1972, p. 42.

Russell, Bertrand. *Marriage and Morals.* New York: H. H. Liveright, 1929.

"The Wedding in the Garden." *Newsweek*, June 21, 1971, pp. 20–21.

"White House Wedding." *Newsweek*, June 14, 1971, pp. 30–34.

for further reading

Customs and Traditions

The Columbia Encyclopedia (in one volume, third edition). Edited by William Bridgewater and Seymour Kurtz. New York and London: Columbia University Press, 1963, *see* "Husband and wife"; "Marriage."

Dugan, George. "Lutherans No Longer Require Brides to Be Given by Fathers." *New York Times*, May 28, 1972, p. 38.

Encyclopaedia Judaica. Jerusalem and New York: The Macmillan Co., 1972, *see* "Marriage."

Fielding, William J. *Strange Customs of Courtship and Marriage.* Garden City, N.Y.: Garden City Books, 1942.

Hunt, Morton M. *The Natural History of Love.* New York: Alfred A. Knopf, Inc., 1959.

Post, Elizabeth L. *Emily Post's Etiquette.* Twelfth revised edition. New York: Funk & Wagnalls, Inc., 1969.

Smith, Bruce L. "Till Death Us Do Part?" *Christianity Today*, Jan. 16, 1970, pp. 5–9.

Sacrament and Contract

Bainton, Roland H. *What Christianity Says about Sex, Love and Marriage.* New York: Association Press, 1957.

Beyle, Marie Henri (Stendhal).... *On Love.* Translated from the French by H. B. V. under the direction of C. K. Scott-Moncrieff. New York: Liveright Publishing Corporation, 1947.

"A Catholic Divorce." *Newsweek*, Aug. 7, 1972, p. 60.

Collier's Encyclopedia. New York: Crowell-Collier Education Corporation, revised annually, *see* "Marriage."

Edmiston, Susan. "How to Write Your Own Marriage Contract." *New York*, Dec. 20–27, 1971, pp. 66–72.

Encyclopaedia Britannica. Chicago: Encyclopaedia Britannica, Inc., revised annually, *see* "Marriage."

Encyclopedia Americana. New York: Americana Corporation, revised annually, *see* "Marriage."

An Encyclopedia of Religion. Edited by Vergilius Ferm. New York: Philosophical Library, Inc., 1945, *see* "Marriage."

Encyclopedia of Religion and Ethics. Edited by James Hastings with the assistance of John A. Selbie and Louis H. Gray. New York: Charles Scribner's Sons, 1951, *see* "Marriage."

Holbrook, David. *The Quest for Love.* London: Methuen & Co., Ltd., 1964.

International Encyclopedia of the Social Sciences. Edited by David L. Sills. New York: The Macmillan Company, 1968, *see* "Marriage."

New Catholic Encyclopedia. New York: McGraw-Hill, Inc., 1967, *see* "Marriage."

The Romance of Tristan and Iseult (as retold by Joseph Bédier). Translated by Hilaire Belloc and completed by Paul Rosenfeld. New York: Pantheon Books, Inc., 1964.

Rougemont, Denis de. *Love in the Western World.* Translated by Montgomery Belgion. New York: Pantheon Books, Inc., 1956.

Prose and Poetry   Lamont, Corliss. *Lover's Credo.* Cranbury, N.J.: A. S. Barnes and Co., Inc., 1972.

Seaburg, Carl (ed.). *Great Occasions: Readings for the Celebration of Birth, Coming-of-Age, Marriage, and Death.* Boston: Beacon Press, 1968.

Silliman, Vincent B., William J. Robbins, and Robert C. Sallies (comps. and eds.). *The Celebration of Marriage.* Norway, Maine: Oxford Hills Press, 1972.

Wilson, Marianne (comp.). *To Love and to Marry: Beautiful Tributes to Love and Marriage.* Illustrated by Gloria Nixon. Kansas City, Mo.: Hallmark Cards, 1971.

Songs and Music

Hodsdon, Nick. *The Raddle of Love: A Collection of New Songs and Hymns and Ideas for Planning Wedding Celebrations, Using Folk Music.* New York: Published privately, 1970. On view at the Sacred Music Library of the Union Theological Seminary, New York City.

"Music to Marry By." *Newsweek,* July 17, 1967, p. 97.

ourownwedding

THE WEDDING OF _____

AND _____

HELD ON _____

AT _____

165

ourown wedding

A Note about the Type   The text of this book was set in Patina, the film version of Palatino,
a type face designed by the noted German typographer Hermann Zapf.
Named after Giovambattista Palatino, a writing master of Renaissance Italy,
Palatino was the first of Zapf's type faces to be introduced to America.
The first designs for the face were made in 1948,
and the fonts for the complete face were issued between 1950 and 1952.
Like all Zapf-designed type faces,
Palatino is beautifully balanced and exceedingly readable.

Composed by University Graphics, Inc., Shrewsbury, New Jersey;
printed by Halliday Lithograph Corporation, West Hanover, Massachusetts;
bound by The Book Press, Inc., Battleboro, Vermont.

Typography and binding design by Clint Anglin.